# Sing a Song of Storytime

By
**Susan M. Dailey**

*Illustrated by*
**Nancy Carroll Wagner**

# Neal-Schuman Publishers, Inc.

*New York*                    *London*

Published by Neal-Schuman Publishers, Inc.
100 William Street, Suite 2004
New York, NY 10038-4512

Printed and bound in the United States of America.

The paper used in this publication meets the minimum requirements of American National Standard for Information Sciences—Permanence of Paper for Printed Library Materials, ANSI Z39.48-1992.

**Library of Congress Cataloging-in-Publication Data**

Dailey, Susan M.
    Sing a song of storytime / by Susan M. Dailey ; illustrated by Nancy Carroll Wagner.
        p.   cm.
    Includes bibliographical references and indexes.
    ISBN-13: 978-1-55570-576-3 (alk. paper)
    ISBN-10: 1-55570-576-6 (alk. paper)
    1. Children's libraries—Activity programs—United States.  2. Children's songs.  I. Title.
Z718.2.U6D35   2007
027.62'5—dc22                                                    2006037544

# Contents

# List of Figures

# Preface

**Sing a Song of Storytime**
*(Sing to "Sing a Song of Sixpence")*

Sing a song of storytime.
I'm so glad you're here!
Sing a song of storytime.
Let's all give a cheer!

With books and songs and fingerplays
We'll have lots of fun.
So get rid of your wiggles and sit very still
'Cause storytime's begun.

Welcome to *Sing a Song of Storytime!* The creative spark for these programs sprung to life with the songs my parents, family, school teachers, librarians, Girl Scout leaders, and camp counselors sang to me as a child. My early enthusiasm grew when I shared these standards with my own children. My many professional years as a librarian who regularly planned and presented storytime programming transformed that early spark into a blaze. I was thrilled with the results when I changed the words to a common tune or wrote my first original composition for a name tag activity. *Sing a Song of Storytime!* reflects many years of successful preschool programs filled with the telling of wonderful stories and the sound of countless children singing.

What role should singing play? As the lyrics above suggest—"With books and songs and fingerplays . . ."—you should never lose sight of the fact that books come first because they are the most important part of the activity. Instilling and nurturing a love for reading and stories is the primary reason that these programs exist. Music is also a key part of almost every program for very good reasons. As anyone who has presented storytimes can attest, music adds more than pizzazz to programs.

Research supports our intuitive impression of music's value to children. "Music optimizes brain development, enhances multiple intelligences, and facilitates bonding between adult and child" (Silberg, 2000: 101). Singing songs assists childhood development of phonological awareness, one of six early literacy pre-reading skills (Whitehurst and Lonigan, 2004). At a purely functional level, music serves several valuable functions in preschool programs. It helps settle a crowd and it allows for the release of pent-up energy. The feeling of familiarity and comfort it engenders has few equals in the early learning environment.

*Sing a Song of Storytime!* celebrates the critical role singing and song play in this learning experience. It suggests several ways to add music to preschool programs, either through recorded music or by singing. The book and companion CD feature more than six dozen choices. I have written the words and arrangements—complete with sheet music—for 32 of these. The others are new lyrics I set to traditional tunes, original chants, and folk or camp songs.

## BOOK ORGANIZATION

In Chapter 1, "Sing a Song of Storytime—Kids, Music, and Programs," I discuss the value of using music with children, ways to incorporate it into programs and tips for "the reluctant vocalist." I have also included information on how I plan, organize and conduct my storytimes. There is an enjoyable alternative to the usual practice of picking a theme and building the elements around it. I explain how to shape a presentation, selecting the various building blocks with my slightly out-of-the-ordinary philosophy about theme-based programming.

The rest of the chapters are a treasure chest of engaging programs linked to flexible themes and arranged by song title. They are filled with fun activities paired with extraordinary picture books and appealing flannel board support materials. These chapters offer a wide array of choices:

- Chapter 2, "Susan's Songbook."
- Chapter 3, "A Fresh Take on Favorites—New Lyrics to Traditional Tunes,"
- Chapter 4, "Traditional Songs, Camp Songs, and Chants,"
- Chapter 5, "Stories that Sing!"—featuring stories with musical refrains, and stories featuring songs.

Chapter 6, "Sources," features bibliographies to support the materials in *Sing a Song of Storytime!* While writing, I posted a request to PUBYAC, a listserv for "Public Libraries, Young Adults and Children," asking for possible titles to include. It's apparent from the number of books suggested and the enthusiasm of the respondents that this type of book is popular with both publishers and program planners. For this reason, my goal was to compile as complete a bibliography as possible. Most of the books included in the bibliography are in print. I also included a few that were published in the past but would likely be in many libraries' collections. Sources cover:

- "singable" picture books,
- recommended recordings,
- print and Internet resources for program planning.

I planned the indices as a handy tool to find a specific item easily, or to use as a cross reference in creating your own distinctive programs. The first lets you search by book titles and authors. The second index is arranged by storytime theme.

## WHAT'S ON THE CD?

*Sing a Song of Storytime!* springs into life with the companion recordings of the songs. It features my singing to most of the songs offered here. Whether you choose to play the tracks for the children or simply listen to prepare for your own performance, I hope you find this feature entertaining and useful.

It is worth noting that I am not a professional musician, and you don't have to be, either. Years ago, I took some piano lessons, played in the junior high band, and sang with the high school choir. Since then, I have had little training, but I love music, especially children's songs. This compilation is my attempt to share this love and these child-tested materials with you.

## PROGRAM ARRANGEMENT

Each of the more than 80 numbered programs is arranged alphabetically, by song. Suggested themes are listed directly below. Next, you will find:

- musical attribution (original or traditional),
- the CD track number location,
- the page number on which sheet music can be found,
- the song—with complete lyrics and directions,
- recommended picture book pairings, and
- tips for success.

Programs also contain graphic elements—usually complementary flannel board figures. I have included many photographs of finished products, and the patterns, with complete directions. Please note that the patterns are easily downloadable from the CD.

All of the picture books I discuss are available for purchase at this time; but be warned, books can go out of print quickly. These are merely suggestions, and I encourage you to use your existing collection to supplement or replace the recommended titles. Sometimes a wonderful book wasn't suggested because it is no longer in print. For example, Frank Asch's *Popcorn* would be a terrific book to use with the "Popcorn" song.

As a librarian, I would like to share these proven materials with others who present storytimes. The intended audience for my book is broader than just librarians. Preschool and early elementary teachers, daycare workers, storytellers and parents will also find useful materials. It will be usable to people of varying experience levels. The novice will find simple and proven materials, while seasoned veterans can find innovative and original compositions to add to their standard repertoire.

I know that *Sing a Song of Storytime* will bring an additional degree of excitement to your programs. I hope that not only children enjoy the music in this book, but that you, too, can tap the joy in singing and the great satisfaction of knowing you are bringing reading and singing together for the children sitting in front of you. J. K. Rowling captures my feelings about music in *Harry Potter and the Sorcerer's Stone*: "Ah, music. A magic beyond all we do here!"

After all, why present songs in a storytime? One answer is that it is a constructive, positive, and practical experience that helps children learn to read and enjoy reading. Another reason? It is enchanting! It is valuable! It is fun!

## REFERENCES

*Every Child Ready to Read @ Your Library Parent Guide*, developed by Dr. Grover C. Whitehurst and Dr. Christopher Lonigan. A Joint Project of the Public Library Association and the Association for Library Service to Children. PLA/ALSC, 2004.

Silberg, Jackie. *125 Brain Games for Toddlers and Twos*. Gryphon House, 2000.

# Acknowledgments

Many people need to be not only acknowledged, but also thanked for helping make this book possible. First, I'd like to express gratitude to my family for encouraging me and for lending their talents. As always, my husband, Doug, was my biggest supporter. Plus, he spent a Saturday scanning all Nancy's patterns while I played with my grandson.

My children were instrumental to this project. Kevin gave up three days of his college spring break to create the accompaniment for the songs. His talent amazes me! He was even willing to sing. Ben mixed and converted the music into a format that could be burnt onto the CD. Stefanie was the first editor and helped me index the manuscript. Jackie graciously lent me Ben, while Caleb, my grandson, was the inspiration for one of the songs. I also want to thank my parents, siblings, Girl Scout leaders and music teachers for singing to and with me. They're the reason I know so many songs.

Nancy Carroll Wagner deserves gratitude and recognition for providing the terrific graphics. She is blessed with incredible talent! And she is so humble about it. I appreciate her ability to produce such wonderful work within a short time frame.

Thanks go to my boss and co-workers, who allowed me to take time off and who have been supportive. They listened when I needed to bounce ideas off someone and when I needed to vent.

I want specifically to acknowledge Meggan Conway from the Lexington Public Library for sharing the "Bingo" idea, and Amy Greiner for letting me use "Earth Song." My gratitude also goes to those "PUBYACkers" who generously suggested titles for the picture book bibliography. They are a most incredible resource!

Michael Kelley, my editor, deserves appreciation for his patience even when I was procrastinating. It was so hard to sit down at the computer sometimes, but he kept nudging me and reminding me that it would be worth it. Everyone I've dealt with at Neal-Schuman has been helpful and friendly. I'd particularly like to thank Charles Harmon, who accepted this proposal and edited my first book. Because of *A Storytime Year,* I've been able to present several workshops, which I absolutely love!

I'd be remiss if I didn't thank all the children, parents, and teachers who have participated in my programs. They are my guinea pigs! And they are so receptive.

My final, but most important, acknowledgment goes to my Heavenly Father who graciously surrounded me with these people and provided these opportunities. I consider music one of His greatest gifts.

# How to Use the Songs and CD

## WHAT'S IN THE SONG CHAPTERS

Songs, songs, and more songs comprise chapters two through four of *Sing a Song of Storytime!*, 80 to be exact. If I had included every song that I've used in storytime throughout the years, the book could be twice as long. In fact, some of my favorite songs are not in the book. How did I decide what to include? Each song contains an original element. All but six of the songs have original lyrics or are totally original compositions. The remaining six folk or camp songs are included because I've created an original visual aid to accompany them.

Although children love "The Wheels on the Bus" and "If You're Happy and You Know It," I didn't add them because they can be found in many other resources. My goal was to share the material that could not be found elsewhere and that had been used successfully in preschool programs. I have listed some of my favorite recordings in the appendix. Some favorites like "Three Little Fishes" and "Three Green and Speckled Frogs" are subject to copyright and therefore could not be included. To find lyrics for many traditional songs, check out Kididdles.com. Terry Kluytmans, the creator of this wonderful resource, has compiled an enormous collection of children's songs. The Musical Mouseum portion includes the songs arranged alphabetically and by subject.

## HOW TO USE THE SONG UNITS

The songs are listed in alphabetical order within each chapter. Planners who don't use themes are encouraged to browse through this section to find a song that appeals to them. If you do theme-based or semi theme-based programs, you should go to the index and find a song that matches your topic.

If the song has a specific storytime function, I indicate this. Song presentation information is included. Tips are also provided for using the songs and for making the visual aid, if there is one. To assist program planners, I suggest at least one picture book to pair with each song.

For the songs where new lyrics were written to a traditional tune, a source for the original melody is listed. Undoubtedly, these could be found on many recordings, but I want to suggest at least one possible choice. Although I tried to match the new lyrics to the original rhythm exactly, it wasn't always possible. Sometimes two notes were substituted for one or vice versa. Other times, I might have changed the accented beat. These adjustments were often made subconsciously so it seemed helpful to include the songs on a CD.

Finding sources for the common tunes led to some interesting discoveries. For instance, I didn't realize that "Ants Go Marching" is sung to "When Johnny Comes Marching Home." I wrote new words to a tune I know as "Did You Ever See a Lassie?" However, I had difficulty finding a source for this song. In my search I discovered that "The More We Get Together" is sung to the same melody. Which came first? I have my theory.

In a personal need for consistency, I suggested a source for "Twinkle, Twinkle Little Star." However, I wanted to write, "If you don't know this tune, you should check out another area of librarianship!" I also could have noted that the same tune is used for "The Alphabet Song," "Baa, Baa, Black Sheep," and "Arabella Miller." Apparently, people have been adding new lyrics to common tunes for a long time.

## HOW TO USE THE CD

The CD contains both audio and graphic files. The primary purpose of the audio tracks is to allow you to learn the music. You are encouraged to listen to the music and then sing it yourself. This is especially true for the name tag activities because you need to pause while the children put their name tags on the board. In some of them, you also need to count the name tags and then sing the next verse with the correct number.

Most of the pieces are sung a cappella. However, the original tunes have accompaniments and are contained in Chapter 2. Many of the accompaniments are simple. Some have a more complex accompaniment, which greatly enhances them. You might want to play these songs during the program, while you and the children sing along. I indicate this in the "Song Presentation" section of the unit.

My son Kevin created the musical accompaniments. He spent much of his college spring break composing them. During a marathon three-day recording session, he connected his keyboard to our computer. Sometimes the musical accompaniment came quickly. Other songs required several attempts before I found one I liked. He is not only talented, but amazingly patient!

The original plan was for the CD to contain just the original tunes, along with the two original story songs. However, I decided to record all the songs after receiving comments that it was sometimes hard to match the new lyrics to the traditional tunes. I realized that sometimes I subconsciously modified the rhythms to fit the words. Hopefully, this decision will benefit everyone who uses *Sing a Song of Storytime!*

When the tracks were finally recorded, my son Ben had to mix the tracks and convert them to MP3 format. This was a family affair! Thanks to Ben, the audio files with accompaniment are recorded in split track format. This means that the voice is on one track, while the accompaniment is on another. If you have a stereo CD player, you will be able to hear just the voice or just the accompaniment by adjusting the left-right balance. The audio files will also play on computers that have the necessary equipment and software.

Some of the songs have patterns so you can make visuals aids. Nancy Carroll Wagner created most of the patterns; a few are mine. You probably won't have difficulty figuring out who created which ones!

The illustrations were scanned and converted to pdf files. Open the files on your computer and print them. The file name matches the pattern list. You could also photocopy the patterns from the book although you might want to enlarge them.

# CD Tracks Play List

1. Apples
2. Building a Snowman
3. Come and Join Our Band
4. Come Join In
5. Frog Surprise
6. I Love Gloves
7. Ice Cream
8. I'll Listen
9. I'm So Mad!
10. It's Almost the Holidays!
11. I've Got Wiggles
12. Kitty Cat, Pounce
13. Little Chicks
14. My Monster
15. Oh, I See a Butterfly
16. Picnic
17. Playing with My Parents
18. Popcorn
19. Rainbow Farm
20. Roll the Snow
21. Searching for My Clothes
22. Something's Hiding in a Flower
23. Spring Flowers
24. Stand Up
25. Strange Thing Happened to Me
26. Three Frogs on a Log
27. Turkey Cheer
28. U.S.A.
29. We Can
30. What Grows in My Garden?
31. Xs and Os
32. Zoo Animals
33. Before I Go to Bed

34. Building a New House
35. Car Sounds
36. Counting Sheep
37. Crayon Box
38. Crayons
39. Do You Have a Ladybug?
40. Do You Know What Time It Is?
41. Fish Tank
42. Hooray for Winter!
43. I Am a Pirate, It's True
44. I Like
45. I'm a School Bus
46. In and Out the Doors
47. Kites
48. My Bike
49. Oh, I Work at the Zoo
50. Oh, Let's Sing a Song of Storytime
51. Penguin Baby
52. Possums
53. Pumpkins, Pumpkins
54. Shaker
55. Sing a Song of Storytime
56. Spring Is Here
57. Summer Is
58. Toolbox
59. Washing the Car
60. Wave Your Rainbow
61. We Are Going on a Bike Ride
62. You're My Friend
63. Little Red Hen

# CHAPTER 1

❧❧❧

# SING A SONG OF STORYTIME—KIDS, MUSIC, AND PROGRAMS

## CHILDREN AND MUSIC: A PERFECT MATCH

- "Babies come into the world with musical preferences. They begin to respond to music while still in the womb. At the age of four months, dissonant notes at the end of a melody will cause them to squirm and turn away. If they like a tune, they may coo."—William J. Cromie, "Harvard Gazette."
- "Before a child can process language, he can process music."—Jackie Silberg, *125 Brain Games for Toddlers and Twos*.

Children and music go together like peanut butter and jelly, Jack and Jill, *Green Eggs and Ham*. Informal observation of my grandson's first year of life reinforces this belief. When he hears music, he bounces up and down. He bobs his head. He vocalizes during singing at church. Even when he doesn't want to nap, lullabies produce droopy eyelids.

Mem Fox states in her book *Reading Magic*, "Songs and rhymes provide comforting rhythms in children's early lives and also expose kids to gorgeous forms of language. They are the natural extension to the heartbeat of the mother and the rhythmic rocking of a child in loving arms or a cradle" (Fox, 2001: 84). She goes on to say, "From songs, children learn words, sentences, rhythm, rhyme, and repetition, all of which they'll find later in the books they read" (Fox, 2001: 85).

When asked about the role of music in the education of young children, Hap Palmer said that the initial goal was to have fun. I agree that enjoyment is an important and obvious value of sharing music with children. He also wanted children to experience how their bodies move with music. Another value that Palmer mentioned was that music helps children realize that not all movement is competitive (Palmer, 1987). This is an interesting and thought provoking benefit of music since our society can be sports obsessed and overly competitive.

In the introduction to *Nurturing Your Child with Music*, John M. Ortiz states, "Because awareness of music and its elements (rhythm, pitch, timber) develops at about the same rate as speech, music can serve as a powerful ally in the development of sound awareness and language skills" (Ortiz, 1999: xv). It can aid in learning, which is witnessed by the speed at which young children memorize nursery rhymes and television commercials. Ortiz also suggests that music can be used as a motivator or to help structure the learning environment. Music has been found to improve general listening skills and to promote expression of feelings (Ortiz, 1999).

A popular theory suggests that playing classical music to babies will increase their IQ. This controversial idea is often referred to as "The Mozart Effect" because of a 1997 book by Don Campbell, which is subtitled "Tapping the Power of Music to Heal the Body, Strengthen the Mind, and Unlock the Creative Spirit." The basic theory is often disputed and even Frances Rauscher, one of the American researchers on the topic, stated that they never claimed that their research proved that listening to Mozart enhances intelligence. Instead, their claims were limited to specific tasks, which related to mental imagery and temporal ordering.

Although the ability to increase intelligence through music isn't definitively proven by quantitative research, collective wisdom indicates that it does have value for children. Through personal experience, I can attest to its specific value in storytime.

## REFERENCES

Cromie, William J. "Music on the Brain: Researchers Explore the Biology of Music." *Harvard Gazette,* March 22, 2001.

*Early Childhood Music Vol. 4, No. 2 Holiday Issue November/December, 1987.* Available: www.happalmer.com/reviews2.htm#EARLY%20CHILDHOOD%20MUSIC

Fox, Mem. **Reading Magic: Why Reading Aloud to Our Children Will Change Their Lives Forever.** Harcourt, 2001.

Ortiz, John M. **Nurturing Your Child with Music: How Sound Awareness Creates Happy, Smart, and Confident Children.** Beyond Words, 1999.

Silberg, Jackie. **125 Brain Games for Toddlers and Twos.** Gryphon House, 2000.

## INCORPORATING MUSIC INTO PROGRAMS

"Music soothes the savage beast" or so goes the often-misquoted line from William Congreve's play *The Mourning Bride.*[1] While I've never actually compared my storytime kids to animals, they do have their "beastly" moments and music is a great way to soothe, entertain and teach them.

There are several ways to use music in preschool programs either through singing or playing recorded music. The first and simplest way is to use music to set a mood. It can be playing when the children first enter the programming area. This is a wonderful opportunity to introduce the children to many terrific children's musicians, especially those whose music isn't likely to be used as part of a program. Some recordings are wonderful to listen to, but don't lend themselves easily to motions or singing along.

Program planners can also use music during craft time. Because this portion of a program often requires parent and child to talk and/or allows parents to share with each other, instrumental music played quietly in the background probably works best. This would be a great opportunity to use classical music or even jazz.

Music can also be used for opening and/or closing activities. Many people who work with young children start programs with a song, such as "If You're Happy and You Know It" or a welcome song. The book includes one original welcome song, "Oh, Let's Sing a Song of Storytime!." I begin storytime with

---

[1] The quote is actually, "Music has charms to soothe the savage breast" and comes from *The Mourning Bride,* act 1, scene 1.

a name tag activity. These are often songs. The words and music, as well as patterns, for several activities appear later in the book. I don't use music for a closing activity during storytime, since we end with crafts. However, I conclude preschool class visits with a closing song. The book contains two.

Quiet-down activities are closely related to opening activities and are another way to incorporate music. These are songs or fingerplays that end with the children's hands in their lap or with them sitting quietly. They can either be used at the beginning of the program or between stories.

Yet another way to use music is as stretches. These songs encourage children to stand and move around. These are often recorded songs and there are certain children's performers, such as Jim Gill, whose music lends itself very well to this type of activity.

The most common way to add music is with participation activities. Many of these could aptly be called "musical fingerplays." Most of the songs in this book fall into this category. Although not necessary, I use visuals with some of them. Patterns and instructions are included.

Another way to add music would be to give the children percussion instruments like tambourines, shakers or rhythm sticks. These could be played along with music and, if desired, the children could march around. The program planner could also play a rhythm and let the children repeat it.

The final and most challenging way to incorporate music in programs is through stories. Some stories include a musical refrain. Some picture books beg to be sung. And some stories can be told entirely in song. The book includes several original stories and a bibliography of "singable" picture books.

When I began compiling the bibliography, I hoped to assemble a complete list of these titles. To this end, I posted a request on the PUBYAC listserv asking for suggestions. It soon became apparent that a complete bibliography would be an impossible task, especially since I wanted to include suggested themes for each book. I limited the bibliography to books currently in print, with the exception of a few titles that were published in the last few years, but have already gone out of print. Illustrated songs are very popular in board book format. I included only a few of these.

Another consideration in compiling the bibliography was whether to include books that could be sung to a certain tune, but weren't necessarily written to be sung. For instance, **Old Black Fly** by Jim Aylesworth could be sung to "Muffin Man" or "Mulberry Bush," with the repetition of certain words. **Mouse's Birthday** by Jane Yolen could also be sung to these same two tunes. June Crebbins' book **Cows in the Kitchen** begs to be sung to "Skip to My Lou," but the book doesn't state that fact. I finally decided not to include this type of book in the bibliography. However, I did suggest tunes for books where a character sang a song, but didn't include a tune, e.g. **In the Rain with Baby Duck** by Amy Hest.

Many books have been converted to song and recorded on CD. Bill Harley sings a version of his book **Sitting Down to Eat** on his CD, *Come Out and Play*. On *Playing Favorites*, Greg and Steve sing a version of Bill Martin's picture book, **Brown Bear, Brown Bear, What Do You See?** to the tune of "Twinkle, Twinkle, Little Star." These were omitted from the bibliography. Books that are packaged with a CD, such as Margaret Read MacDonald's **A Hen, a Chick, and a String Guitar**, were included.

Similarly, many videos have adapted picture books to song. Two that come to mind are *Antarctic Antics*, based on the poetry book by Judy Sierra and Lois Ehlert's picture book **Waiting for Wings**. Both were produced by Weston Woods, but neither is in the bibliography.

The bibliography has over 100 titles, even with these omissions. If you love "singable" books, you should find a few new titles to add to your repertoire.

Librarians, teachers, daycare workers, and parents who've never used music with children are encouraged to start small. They can begin by using music to set a mood or by singing a simple song they remember from their own childhood. Incorporating music into programs isn't difficult, and is truly a valuable addition.

## ENCOURAGING TIPS FOR RELUCTANT SINGERS

Several years ago, I attended a seminar where the speak asked everyone who was able to sing to raise his or her hand. Very few people did so. She went on to say that everyone's hand should be in the air. She pointed out that she hadn't asked if we could star in a Broadway musical or even if we would sing a solo with a church choir. Some people carry a tune better than others; but if we have the ability to vocalize, we can sing. And the ability required to use the material in this book doesn't demand an accomplished singer, for several reasons.

First, preschool children are a non-critical audience. They are not evaluating your ability. Besides, they should be singing along with you. If you are enthusiastic, they will be, too!

Adults attending your program can certainly be more intimidating. Again, your attitude is the key. Don't focus your attention on the adults, and don't try to guess what they are thinking. Instead, focus on the children and the material. Encourage the caregivers to participate. Make the experience fun!

Second, the music in this book isn't opera. I hope you'll already be familiar with some of the songs, or the tunes, where new lyrics were written for old melodies. For the original compositions, there is basic sheet music and an accompanying CD. The primary purpose of this CD is to teach the songs to those program planners who don't read music.

The third reason you can use the material in this book relates to the accompanying CD. If you really aren't comfortable singing, you can use recorded music. I recommend that you sing along, though. Don't use recorded music to replace your voice, just to supplement it.

Although there are many wonderful artists and recordings available, I prefer to sing myself. Using a CD or tape player adds complications to the program, e.g. finding a convenient electrical outlet or making sure the batteries work. It can also slow down your ability to move quickly from one activity to the next, especially if you are using a cassette. In this case, you should have the tape forwarded to the correct spot.

Singing without a tape has other advantages. I can easily vary the volume and tempo of the song. For example, when I use a repetitive song like "Five Little Ducks," the second verse might be sung very loudly, while the third might be whispered. In a song like "A Ram Sam Sam," I will sing the song repeatedly, getting a little faster each time. I can also pause, either for dramatic effect or to allow the children to fill in a word.

A final word—if you aren't comfortable singing and can't find recorded music, you can always chant the lyrics. Many of the original songs in this book began as spoken fingerplays. Feel free to return them to this format if that's what it takes to make them useable for you.

## PLANNING PROGRAMS

Planning is one key to having a successful preschool program. Before developing the actual programs, planners need to consider their philosophy about theme-based programs. There are convincing arguments for and against them. After this decision is made, planners should also determine their personal style in regard to structuring programs. You may prefer to plan the order of the program in advance, as I do. On the other hand, you might be comfortable making decisions spontaneously during the program.

### Value of Themes

When I wrote my previous book, *A Storytime Year*, I was an avid proponent of "pure" theme-based programs. All the books and activities in my programs related to some specific theme. I also believed very strongly in the value of participation. A few years ago, I realized that these two beliefs don't always mesh well. It occurred to me that children couldn't fully participate in the fingerplays and songs if they were different each week. This led me to alter my opinion about theme-based programs. I now use what I refer to as "semi theme-based programs." Simply put, the books and craft projects are theme-based, but not all the activities are.

Why present theme-based programs at all? For the same reasons I mentioned in *A Storytime Year:* A theme gives boundaries within which to select materials. There are dozens, if not hundreds, of good stories on any theme that could be shared; themes help narrow the choices. In addition, themes selected in relation to specific times of year provide children with an organized introduction to our culture and natural world. Personally speaking, themes provide a challenge—the quest to locate appropriate materials—and satisfaction, when the program comes together.

Whether you choose to use themes or not should be a personal decision. However, those who don't use theme-based programs should not limit their stories to only the most recently published titles. If they do, they will deprive children of many wonderful older books. ***Green Eggs and Ham*** is a new book to a three-year old who is hearing it for the first time. Choosing only new titles ignores the fact that storytime audiences are constantly changing.

Using "semi theme-based programs" has proven to be a successful change in my storytimes. However, I still plan "true theme-based programs" for eight preschool and kindergarten classes each month. It is worth finding—or writing—activities when I will use them this many times. Realistically, children wouldn't learn fingerplays and songs that they only hear once a month. The appendix includes a bibliography of resources for program planning. This will help program planners who want all the activities to be theme related, although I highly recommend you consider trying "semi theme-based programs."

## Semi Theme-Based Programs

My method for planning begins by choosing a theme for each week of the month. Then I select books and a craft related to the specific themes. Occasionally I'll choose a magnetic/flannel board story, video or game. For the participation activities, I decide upon one fingerplay or song that corresponds to each of the chosen themes for the month. These are the activities that will be used every week during the month. In addition, I choose a name tag activity and a quiet-down song or fingerplay for the month.

For the parents, I make up a sheet with the words/lyrics for the month's activities on one side. The other side includes the themes for the month, storytime expectations, and other pertinent information. They can also share the activities at home with the children. See Figure 1-1 and 1-2 for a sample fingerplay sheet.

I've found several advantages to "semi theme-based programs." The first was mentioned previously. The children learn the songs and fingerplays; therefore, they can easily participate in them. More importantly, research has shown that repetition increases brain connections and is essential for learning. A further advantage is that the actual program moves more quickly because new activities don't have to be taught each week.

There are advantages for the program planner, as well. It reduces the amount of time spent planning. Finding several good activities for a theme is usually more difficult than locating books. Now I only have to find one great activity per theme.

Although program planners don't have to memorize the songs and fingerplays, it helps greatly. At the very least, you need to be thoroughly familiar with the fingerplays and songs. Using the same activities for several weeks assists with this.

# Fingerplays & Songs

## Spring Flowers

It is spring!
Let's plant some seeds.
Here comes the sun
And rain they need.

Wait awhile
And they will grow.
Little blue flowers
In a row.

Repeat with pink and white flowers

## Three Frogs on a Log

Three frogs on a log
One fly in the sky
Buzzzzzzzz

One fly flies nearby
Those three frogs on a log
Then, zip, zap, gulp
Splash.

Repeat with two, then one.

## Books

Big books, little books,
  (hold hands out wide, bring together)
Short books, tall
  (hold 1 hand above other, spread apart)
Thin books, fat books,
  (hold thumb and pointer close together, spread apart)
I love them all.
  (place hand over heart)

April 2006-Ossian Branch

## Open, Shut Them

Open, shut them,
  (open and close hands in front of you)
Open, shut them,
Give a little clap clap clap.
  (clap 3 times as you say "clap")
Open, shut them, open, shut them,
Lay them in your lap.

## Spring Is Here
(sung to "Are You Sleeping?")

I see flowers,
  (place one open hand on top of other palm, wiggle fingers)
I see bird's nests,
  (cup hand)
Butterflies,
  (touch palms with fingers pointing outward, move hands)
Rainy skies.
  (flutter fingers downward)
Everything is growing,
  (move hands upward)
The wind is gently blowing.
  (move hands back and forth in waving motion & blow)
Spring is here!
Spring is here!

## My Bike
(sung to "The Farmer in the Dell")

Pedal round and round,
  (roll hands around each other)
Pedal round and round,
I steer my bike
  (pretend to steer)
Anywhere I like.
Pedal round and round

**Figure 1-1   Sample Fingerplay sheet**

April 2006

Dear Parent,

The Ossian Branch Library is pleased to have your child enrolled in our Storytime.   During the month we will use the activities on the other side of the paper each week. You can help by talking about the week's theme and practicing our fingerplays and songs with your child.

The dates and themes for this session are:

|  |  |
|---|---|
| April 3 & 4 | I Love My Library |
| April 10 & 11 | Hooray for Spring! |
| April 17 & 18 | Frog Frenzy |
| April 24 & 25 | We're Going on a Bike Ride |

Stories will begin at 1:30 on Mondays or 10:30 a.m. on Tuesdays in the Meeting Room. Please make every effort to be on time since late arrivals are very disruptive.  Our Storytime will last about 30 minutes so we won't be able to wait on late arrivals or repeat beginning activities.  Please sit with your child beside or in front of you and participate even if your child is shy.  You are the best role model!

We do not expect rapt, silent attention; however, if your child becomes very disruptive you may wish to remove them from the room until they calm down.

Please be aware that if Northern Wells is cancelled due to weather, there will be no Storytime on Monday afternoon.   If Northern Wells has a delay or closing on Tuesday, Storytime will be cancelled.

With the hectic pace of life, you are to be commended for giving your child this experience. It is my hope that the children will enjoy Storytime now and will always view books and the library as an important part of their lives.

Looking forward to a fun time,

**Susan**

**Figure 1-2    Sample Storytime letter**

## ORGANIZING THE ELEMENTS

When planning a preschool program, I determine the order in which the materials will be used. This allows me to move quickly from one segment to the next. I use the following basic outline:

Name tag activity

Quiet down fingerplay/song

> Book
>
> Participation activities
>
> Magnetic or prop story or book
>
> Participation activities
>
> Book or video
>
> Craft

> Below is a program that uses a theme and materials from the sample fingerplay sheet.

> SPRING (theme)
>
> Spring Flowers—name tag activity
>
> Open, Shut Them—quiet down fingerplay
>
> *Spring Song* by Barbara Seuling
>
> Spring is Here—song
>
> "Because It Was Spring" by Susan M. Dailey, page 50 in *A Storytime Year*—magnetic story
>
> Books—fingerplay
>
> My Bike—song
>
> *Cold Little Duck, Duck, Duck* by Lisa Westberg Peters
>
> Three Frogs on a Log—song with prop
>
> *Mouse's First Spring* by Lauren Thompson (if time allows)
>
> Thumbprint Pictures—craft, page 40 in *A Storytime Year*

The schedule can vary, depending on the length of stories and activities, but my storytime always begins with a name tag activity and ends with a craft. I don't always use the quiet down fingerplay in the same location, however. Instead I utilize it at the point in the program where I think the children might need to settle down, such as after an activity that has them moving around.

As mentioned previously, I also plan a program for eight preschool and kindergarten classes each month. For these groups I eliminate the name tag activity and replace the craft with a closing song. "Do You Know What Time It Is?" and "Stand Up" are the two original closing songs in the book.

## Name Tag Activities

Although I refer to this as a name tag activity, the term might be misleading. I used to give the children name tags, but some either wouldn't wear the tags, or played with them during the program. Now the name tags are laminated paper with a magnet on the back. They are usually in the shape of a simple object, often seasonally related.

When the children first get to the programming room, they find their name tags. To start storytime, we sing a song or recite a fingerplay in which each child is asked to put his name tag on the magnetic board.

If the children aren't wearing name tags during the program, why have them at all? Name tags help me learn the children's names. I see the names when I lay them out. I get to associate the children with their names when they put them on the board. I also use the name tags to take attendance at the end of the program. In addition, the children enjoy putting the name tags on the board. They also identify their names in print, which is a valuable preschool skill.

Some name tag activities require the children to come up in a specific order based on the color or type of their name tag. Other times the children may bring up their name tags in any order. Some children might not be comfortable coming forward the first few weeks, especially toddlers. While I encourage them, I do not pressure them to participate. We clap each time a group of children puts their name tags on the board. We often count the number of name tags, which reinforces this essential preschool skill.

There are several songs in the book that can be used as name tag activities. They can be easily located by using the subject index. However, these activities can be used even if you don't intend to have name tags or prefer for the children to wear them. Some planners use these at the end to gather the name tags from the children. The songs can also be used as simple participation activities. You can give each child a shape, which they will bring to the board at the appropriate time. Although this might not sound exciting, children enjoy placing objects on the board.

### Quiet Down Fingerplays

The quiet down fingerplay/song is one that ends with the children sitting quietly. I would recommend that all storytime planners memorize one or two. The book includes several songs that serve this function. They can be found using the subject index. You can also utilize other techniques to settle a group, e.g. whispering, a hand signal, etc.

### Books

Sharing literature is the basis of any storytime. We are fortunate to live in a time when there are so many wonderful picture books on such a large variety of themes.

Several things need to be considered when selecting books, especially the age of the listening children. Obviously, not all wonderful picture books make great read-alouds. I believe that listening to a story in a group situation is a different and more advanced skill than one-on-one reading. It requires the children to be able to focus their attention beyond themselves and their immediate space. For this reason, I usually choose short, fast paced stories, and I typically read the longest book first.

My favorite storytime books allow the children to participate in some manner. This can be through a repetitive refrain, sound effects, motions, etc. The books are usually humorous, with simple, predictable plots. Picture books in rhyme or with strong rhythm are terrific choices. Some beginning readers and nonfiction titles work well in storytime.

Audience age isn't just a factor in regard to the length of the stories. It also pertains to subject matter. Certain kinds of humor and abstract storylines aren't effective with very young children.

When it comes to illustrations, ideally they will be both large and uncluttered. However, smaller books can work if the pictures aren't busy. Conversely, a large book like **Where's Waldo?** by Martin Handford is much too detailed to share with a group. You also need to be aware of how dependent the story is upon the illustrations. If children must be able to see clearly small details in the illustrations, you must either point them out, or leave the book to be shared in a one-on-one situation.

### Participation Activities

The participation activities in my programs include fingerplays and games, as well as songs. However, as stated earlier, this book concentrates on music. You can use the "Resources for Program Planning" section of the sources to find fingerplays. Often more than one activity is used between stories.

The sample program above utilizes the "semi theme-based" philosophy so the activities will remain the same throughout the month. Occasionally, I will add a game that relates specifically to the week's theme and is only used for that week. In the case of the sample program, I might add "Spring Sequencing" from page 44 of *A Storytime Year*. This game has the children help arrange illustrations in the correct sequential order.

### Magnetic and Prop Stories

I often use a magnetic or prop story in the middle of a program, especially for the monthly preschool visits. These stories come from many sources, including my earlier book *A Storytime Year*. This book includes five stories with a musical, repetitive refrain. I've also written three story songs.

Because these stories are usually told rather than read, they require more preparation. The stories I select usually have a very simple, predictable plot. With the exception of the stories told entirely in song, I don't memorize them word for word.

### Videos

I try to show a video every two to three weeks. Although most children watch videos at home, they don't usually see the short, literature-based videos for which libraries have public performance rights. Although I consider myself an expressive reader, I don't measure up to to Meryl Streep, who narrates the video version of *Chrysanthemum* by Kevin Henkes. Nor can my rendition of the Judy Sierra's poetry in *Antarctic Antics* compare to the musical versions on that video. Some stories, especially those that are wordless or almost wordless, work better in video format than as group read-alouds.

Generally speaking, I've found the most successful videos for preschoolers are either live-action or animated. Many videos are done in a style called iconographic. Basically, still photographs of illustrations from a picture book are shown with a narrator reading the story. Preschoolers seem to have trouble focusing on this type of video for any length of time.

### Crafts

For many years my library has ended storytime with a craft. There are many valid arguments against doing crafts at storytime. Money must be budgeted for supplies or they must be donated. Crafts can be messy and require space for the children to work. The library staff often needs to do some preparatory work.

Despite these problems, we do crafts for several reasons. Children enjoy them. They appreciate having a visible reminder of their participation in storytime. This might be the only opportunity for some children to work at crafts, especially those that use special supplies. Crafts encourage creativity.

## PRESENTING PROGRAMS

What is the correct way to conduct a storytime program? I wish I had "the" answer. The reality is that there isn't just one right way to do it. It depends on many variables. It depends on the physical situation. It depends on the audience and community. It depends on the programmer's personality and style. The following tips come from personal experience and from the generous sharing of others in workshops, conference sessions and on PUBYAC, a listserv for children's and young adult librarians.

### Be Prepared

I've found that being prepared—both mentally and physically—is necessary to have a successful program. When I'm prepared, I'm comfortable with the program. This allows me to focus on engaging the children and on delivering the material with enthusiasm.

Being mentally prepared doesn't mean taking a tranquilizer before a program! It means having a positive attitude and realistic expectations.

Your attitude will determine the atmosphere in a program. Some program planners are very exuberant, while others are nurturing. Both can be very successful, although the mood will be different in their programs.

It isn't reasonable to expect young children to sit quietly and be totally attentive for long periods of time. Children have different temperaments and will respond differently to situations. Group dynamics will affect your programs. As the expression goes, "Expect the unexpected!"

You also need to have realistic expectations for yourself. You need to realize that some programs will go better than others. You need to know that certain aspects get easier with experience. You also need to accept the fact that programs can be exhilarating, but physically and mentally exhausting. Burnout is a reality for program planners and you need strategies to combat it. Maybe it means taking a few weeks off between sessions. Attending conferences and workshops also helps. For me, writing a new story, song or fingerplay is what recharges my enthusiasm.

As I noted above, my personal style includes planning the order for my programs in advance. I don't always follow the outline exactly, but it helps me feel prepared. Some planners require less structured preparation than I do. I envy those who can work "off the cuff" and conduct a successful program. Awareness of your personal style is part of being mentally prepared.

Another aspect of preparation is knowing your material. Unfortunately, I've learned this through experience. I won't bore you with examples, except to say that one involved a black and white film that I believe was in Czech!

Physical preparation means having the materials within easy reach and making sure all the pieces for flannel/magnetic stories are in order. This allows the program to move quickly and smoothly. Because my programs are presented in the meeting room, I sometimes have to rearrange the space to meet my needs.

### Encourage Participation

I've found that participation is another aspect of successful programs. As stated earlier, my favorite storytime books include an element of participation. Some books allow obvious participation. With others, participation can be added. If a character is preparing for bed, for instance, the children might mime some of the motions of brushing teeth, getting a drink, etc. Not all stories benefit from participation, however.

Fingerplays, songs and games are the primary opportunity for participation in a program. As mentioned above, I switched to "semi theme-based programs" to allow the children to participate in the fingerplays and songs more fully. If adults attend the program, encourage them to participate also. We say in our storytime letter, "Please sit with your child beside or in front of you and participate even if your child is shy. You are the best role model!"

I scatter the activities throughout the program. However, some planners use fingerplays and songs at the beginning and then read all the stories. Others save all their activities for the end. Although I obviously prefer my method, there isn't one correct way to do it. You'll have to decide what works best for you and your audience.

### Maintain Crowd Control

Does this phrase conjure up visions of police in protective vests with riot gear? This certainly isn't what I'm talking about; but to conduct successful programs, you need to establish a level of control. One extreme would be to expect the children and adults, if any are present, to sit absolutely still, never moving or uttering a sound. The other extreme is absolute chaos, with each child and parent doing exactly as he or she pleases. Obviously, neither end of the continuum is desirable or realistic.

Your goal is to decide where you are comfortable and to establish that level. You then need to communicate your expectations to the children. I don't have a formal list of rules and expectations. You might find it helpful to do so. However, the list shouldn't be too long. I read somewhere that the number of rules should be limited to the age of the children. Another recommendation I have heard is that the rules should come from the group. I believe that would work well with a consistent group, such as a class. However, attendance at my programs varies greatly. Someone suggests posting the rules, even though most of the children can't read. (Perhaps you could find pictures that would symbolize them.) They should be presented in positive terms, e.g. "Listen quietly during stories," instead of "Don't talk during stories." Some situations can and should be ignored. As in parenting, you need to pick your battles. Praise and encourage positive behavior.

Our storytime letter states, "We do not expect rapt, silent attention; however, if your child becomes very disruptive, you may wish to remove them from the room until they calm down." This clearly applies to programs where adults are present. You might prefer that adults do not attend the programs. Teresa, a colleague, says she has fewer problems because she doesn't have the parents in the room. I maintain that I have fewer problems because the adults are there. This is yet another area that doesn't have one correct answer.

Prevention is the best way to deal with discipline issues. Our programs are conducted in a separate area. If this isn't possible, try to limit the distractions. This might mean removing toys or books from the area, facing the children in a specific direction, etc. I have the children wait in the children's department until the program begins and we enter the storytime area as a group. Rituals help establish that the program is beginning and are particularly important if you don't have a separate area.

Careful preparation also prevents some situations. Many discipline problems occur during transitioning or "down times," so being able to move quickly throughout the program helps. You will need a plan to re-establish control. This is especially true if you are using highly physical activities. Variety and participation help prevent boredom, and less boredom leads to fewer control issues.

As much as we wish, hope and plan, problems will occur. What do you do when they happen? Once again, it depends on the situation, on the child, on your style.

Although none of these are innovative ideas, here are a few specific suggestions. If a group is getting loud, try whispering. Increasing your volume often causes the group to get louder. Sometimes it is enough to wait. Silence can speak volumes! Occasionally, you need to give a child the "mom/teacher" look. Be positive, but firm. At times children are too comfortable with a situation. In that case, shaking up the routine might help. Some ongoing problems require talking specifically and directly to a child or adult. It is best to do this before or after the program and away from others.

I encourage you to ask colleagues for advice and support. Sometimes it's enough to receive sympathy and to realize that your problems aren't unique. Sometimes we need to remind ourselves of the importance of what we do. On the *Just Read, Florida* website, Governor Jeb Bush writes, "Children are precious gifts and the opportunity to inspire the love of reading is both a great honor and an extraordinary responsibility."

# CHAPTER 2

# SUSAN'S SONGBOOK

**1. APPLES**

**Words and music by Susan M. Dailey**                                   **Apples (Food), Fall**

CD Track 1

Sheet Music, see page 14

### Song Presentation

This is a Name Tag Activity.

Make a name tag for each child using the patterns from "Five Green Apples" on page 151.

Learn the song by listening to the CD or by playing the sheet music.

As you sing the song, have the children bring their name tags to the magnetic/flannel board at the end of the appropriate verse.

### Apples

Juicy, red apples
Hanging on the trees:
Yummy in my tummy—
Bring me some, please.

Sweet, yellow apples
Hanging on the trees:
Yummy in my tummy—
Bring me some, please.

Tart, green apples
Hanging on the trees:
Yummy in my tummy—
Bring me some, please.

### Tips

- Variations

    - This song can also be used as a "between book" activity by giving the children one of each color apple. Change the last line to "Hold it up, please," and the children can hold up the appropriate color apple.

### Picture Book Pairings

Ehlert, Lois. *Leaf Man*. Illustrated by author. Harcourt, 2005. A man made of leaves blows away, traveling wherever the wind may take him. (Fall)

Marzollo, Jean. *I Am an Apple*. Illustrated by Judith Moffat. Scholastic, 1997. Depicts a bud on an apple tree as it grows into an apple, ripens, is harvested, and provides seeds as a promise for the future. (Apples)

### Patterns Needed

- Apple pattern

### Visual Aid Creation

1. See page 151 / CD file 4-46 for the pattern. Download and print .pdf files or photocopy them.
2. Trace the pattern on red, yellow and green paper.
3. Put magnets on the back.

Figure 2-1   Apples sheet music

## 2. BUILDING A SNOWMAN

**Words and music by Susan M. Dailey**                                    **Winter**

CD Track 2

Sheet Music, see page 16

## Song Presentation

You might want to sing along with the CD for this song.

Have the children act out the motions as indicated.

## Building a Snowman

Take some snow and roll it around.
  (*Roll hands around each other.*)
Around, around, around, around, around, around, around
Around, around, around, around, around, around, around
Around, around, around, around, around, around, around
'Til you have a huge ball.
  (*Show "large" circle with hands.*)

Then take some snow and roll it around.
  (*Roll hands around each other.*)
Around, around, around, around, around, around, around
Around, around, around, around, around, around, around
'Til you have a big ball.
  (*Show "big" circle with hands.*)

Then take some snow and roll it around.
  (*Roll hands around each other.*)
Around, around, around, around, around, around, around
'Til you have a small ball.
  (*Show "small" circle with hands.*)

Now add two eyes, a nose and a hat.
  (*Point to eyes, nose and top of head.*)
And wrap around a scarf and that is that!
  (*Pretend to wrap scarf, slap palms together in up and down motion.*)

## Tips

- Variations

  - You can create a visual aid to go along with the song, using the instructions below.

- The **Snowy Day** is available in video form in *The Ezra Jack Keats Library*, or *The Caldecott Video Library*, Volume 3, both available from Weston Woods.

## Picture Book Pairings

Keats, Ezra Jack. **The Snowy Day**. Illustrated by author. Viking, 1996. A little boy discovers the many joys that can be experienced in the snow in this classic story, which won the Caldecott Medal.

### Visual Aid Creation

To make the visual aid, buy the following:

3 Styrofoam balls in different sizes—6 inches, 5 inches, and 4 inches

Styrofoam sheet for base

Dowel rod

Animal eyes with shank

Orange bump chenille

Fabric

Doll hat

1. Cut the dowel rod approximately 16" long.
2. Using a dowel rod, make a hole through the center of the balls. Flatten one side of the smallest ball by pushing on a flat surface. Flatten both sides of largest and middle ball. This allows the balls to sit better on each other.
3. Cut one section of the bump chenille to make a "carrot nose." Cut a piece of fabric for the scarf. I used fleece.
4. Put the dowel rod into the Styrofoam sheet base. As you sing the song, at the end of the first three verses thread the balls onto the rod. During the last verse, push the shanks of the animal eyes and the bump chenille into the small ball. Then put the doll hat on top and wrap the scarf fabric around the top of the middle ball. I used a straw hat, but other styles are available.

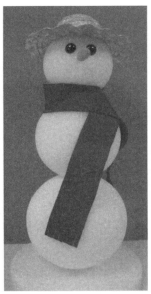

Figure 2-2   Snowman photo

Figure 2-3   Building a Snowman sheet music

## 3. COME AND JOIN OUR BAND

**Words and music by Susan M. Dailey**                    **Music, Sounds**

CD Track 3
Sheet Music, see page 18

### Song Presentation

This is a Name Tag Activity.

Make name tags for each child using the patterns on page 18.

Learn the song by listening to the CD or by playing the sheet music.

As you sing the song, have the children bring their name tags to the magnetic/flannel board at the end of the appropriate verse.

After each instrument, count the number on the board. Sing the next verse filling in the correct number. I sang sample verses on the CD.

### Come and Join Our Band

Come and join our band,
the best in all the land.
So, if you have a trumpet,
a toot, toot, toot, toot, trumpet,
come and join our band.

Come and join our band,
the best in all the land.
Now we have———trumpets,
———toot, toot, toot, toot, trumpets,
Don't we sound just grand?

Continue with rat-a-tat-tat drums and strum, strum, strum guitars.

### Tips

- Variations

    - You can also have the children march around and pretend to play the trumpet and drum. Because the guitar is not common in a marching band, I have the kids dance around while they pretend to play it. You might want to omit the second verses about each instrument.

### Picture Book Pairings

Moss, Lloyd. *Zin! Zin! Zin! A Violin*. Illustrated by Marjorie Priceman. Simon & Schuster, 1995. Ten instruments take their parts one by one in a musical performance. (Music)

Wolff, Ferida. *It Is the Wind*. Illustrated by James Ransome. HarperCollins, 2005. At night the sounds of various animals lull a child to sleep. (Sounds)

## Patterns needed

**Figure 2-4 Trumpet**

**Figure 2-5 Drum**

**Figure 2-6 Guitar**

## Visual Aid Creation

1. See the patterns above / CD files 2-4 through 2-6. Download and print .pdf files or photocopy them.
2. Color the instruments.
3. Put magnets on the back.
4. Write the children's names in the blank space beside the instruments.

**Figure 2-7 Come and Join Our Band sheet music**

## 4. COME JOIN IN

**Words and music by Susan M. Dailey**                    **Movement**

CD Track 4

Sheet Music, see page 20

### Song Presentation

This is a stretch activity, so the children have a chance to move around between stories.

Learn the song by listening to the CD or by playing the sheet music.

Sing a line and have the children repeat it.

Have the children move as indicated.

### Come Join In

Say what I say.
Come join in.
Do what I do.
Now, let's begin.

Hop, hop, hop, hop,
touch the ground.
Shake, shake, shake, shake.
Now, twirl around.

March, march, march, march,
Pretend to sneeze.
Twist, twist, twist, twist.
Now, sit down please.

### Tips

• On the third line of the song, make some kind of motion and encourage the children to repeat it.

### Picture Book Pairings

Harter, Debbie. *The Animal Boogie*. Illustrated by author. Barefoot, 2000. In the jungle, the animals' toes are twitching, their bodies are wiggling, and their wings are flapping—as they teach children how to do the Animal Boogie.

**Come Join In**

Susan M. Dailey

Figure 2-8  Come Join In sheet music

## 5. FROG SURPRISE

**Words and music by Susan M. Dailey**                    **Frogs, Bedtime**

CD Track 5

Sheet Music, see page 22

### Song Presentation

You might want to sing along with the CD for this song.

Have the children move as indicated.

### Frog Surprise

Late last night I had a surprise!
(*Throw hands in air.*)

It was green with bulgy eyes,
  (*Make circles with hands and put in front of eyes.*)
with hopping legs. "Ribbit, ribbit," it said.
  (*Point to legs, make "ribbit" sounds.*)
I found a frog on my bed.

And it went hop, hoppity, hop.
  (*Hop fingers.*)
Yes, it went hop, hoppity, hop.
And it went hop, hoppity, hop.
Yes, it went hop, hoppity, hop.
I frowned at the frog and shook my head.
  (*Frown, shake head.*)
"You don't belong on my bed!
  (*Shake finger.*)
Go back home," I told that frog
  (*Point backward with thumb over shoulder.*)
So it hopped right back to its bog.
  (*Hop fingers.*)

## Tips

- Variation

  - You can also have the children stand up and hop around.
  - You might want to repeat the "hopping" section several times.
  - Finish with the children hopping back to their places and sitting down.

## Picture Book Pairings

Asher, Sandy. *Too Many Frogs*. Illustrated by Keith Graves. Philomel, 2005. Rabbit's comfortable nightly routine is disturbed by exuberant Froggie, who settles in for a snack and a story without being invited. (Frogs)

Dewdney, Anna. *Llama Llama Red Pajama*. Illustrated by author. Viking, 2005. At bedtime, a little llama worries after his mother puts him to bed and goes downstairs. (Bedtime)

**Figure 2-9  Frog Surprise sheet music**

## 6. I LOVE GLOVES

**Words and music by Susan M. Dailey**                                     **Winter, Clothes**

CD Track 6

Sheet Music, see page 24

### Song Presentation

Make clothing pieces using the patterns on page 24.

Give each child one kind of glove and then either a hat, boots, scarf or snowsuit card.

Have them hold up each card on the appropriate word.

When you sing "I love gloves," all the kids should hold up their glove cards.

You might want to sing along with the CD for this song.

### I Love Gloves

I like hats and I like boots.
I like scarves and warm snowsuits,
but I love gloves!

Gloves of white with polka dots,
gloves of pink with purple spots.
Yes, I love gloves!

Gloves of red with stripes of blue,
gloves of green and yellow, too.
Yes, I love gloves!

### Picture Book Pairings

Chodos-Irvine, Margaret. *Ella Sarah Gets Dressed*. Illustrated by author. Harcourt, 2003. Despite the advice of others in her family, Ella Sarah persists in wearing the striking and unusual outfit of her own choosing. (Clothes)

Kuskin, Karla. *Under My Hat I Have a Hood*. Illustrated by Fumi Kosaka. HarperCollins, 2004. A child describes the many layers of clothing needed to brave the winter weather. (Winter)

## Patterns Needed

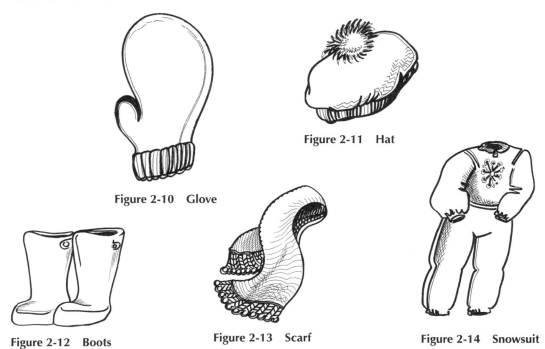

Figure 2-11    Hat

Figure 2-10    Glove

Figure 2-12    Boots

Figure 2-13    Scarf

Figure 2-14    Snowsuit

## Visual Aid Creation

1. See above patterns / CD files 2-10 through 2-14. Download and print .pdf files or photocopy them.
2. Color the gloves in the four different ways indicated in the song.

Figure 2-15    I Love Gloves sheet music

## 7. ICE CREAM

**Words and music by Susan M. Dailey**                    **Food, Summer, Colors**

CD Track 7

Sheet Music, see page 26

### Song Presentation

This is a Name Tag Activity.

Make a name tag for each child, using the patterns on page 26.

Learn the song by listening to the CD or by playing the sheet music.

As you sing the song, have the children bring their name tags to the magnetic/flannel board at the end of the appropriate verse.

### Ice Cream

Ice cream! Ice cream!
Yummy, yummy ice cream!
All colors of the rainbow.

Who has ice cream
that is colored pink?
Put it on the board.

(Continue with yellow, green and white.)

### Picture Book Pairings

Hutchins, Pat. *The Doorbell Rang*. Illustrated by author. Greenwillow, 1986. Each time the doorbell rings, there are more people who have come to share Ma's wonderful cookies. (Food)

Nikola-Lisa, W. *Summer Sun Risin'*. Illustrated by Don Tate. Lee & Low, 2002. An African American boy enjoys a summer day on his family's farm, milking the cows, fishing, and having fun. (Summer)

Wood, Audrey. *The Deep Blue Sea*. Illustrated by Bruce Wood. Scholastic, 2005. Introduces various colors by presenting a colorful scene on a rock in the deep blue sea. (Colors)

## Patterns Needed

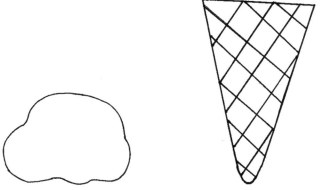

Figure 2-16   Ice Cream Scoop        Figure 2-17   Ice Cream Cone

## Visual Aid Creation

1.  See patterns above / CD files 2-16 through 2-17. Download and print .pdf files or photocopy them.
2.  Trace the pattern for the ice cream on pink, yellow, green, and white paper.
3.  Photocopy the pattern for the cone on brown paper.
4.  Assemble the pieces.
5.  Put magnets on the back.

Figure 2-18   Ice Cream sheet music

## 8. I'LL LISTEN

**Words and music by Susan M. Dailey**                                    **Body**

CD Track 8
Sheet Music, see page 28

### Song Presentation

This is a Quiet Down Activity.

Learn the song by listening to the CD or by playing the sheet music.

### I'll Listen

I'll listen, I'll listen with my nose. Oh, no! (*spoken*)
  (*Point to various body parts.*)
I'll listen, I'll listen with my toes. Oh, no! (*spoken*)
I'll listen, I'll listen with my shoulders. Oh, no! (*spoken*)
What will I listen with? My ears!

I'll look and I'll look with my tongue. Oh, no! (*spoken*)
I'll look and I'll look with my hips. Oh, no! (*spoken*)
I'll look and I'll look with my belly button. Oh, no! (*spoken*)
What will I look with? My eyes!

I'll think and I'll think with my teeth. Oh, no! (*spoken*)
I'll think and I'll think with my knees. Oh, no! (*spoken*)
I'll think and I'll think with my hair. Oh, no! (*spoken*)
What will I think with? My brain!

So if you are ready to think with your brain,
And if you are ready to look with your eyes,
And if you are ready to listen with your ears,
Then we are ready for storytime. Shhhh!
  (*Slow down and get quieter.*)

### Tips

- On the first line, you might ask the children if they really listen with their noses before you sing "Oh, no!"
- You can really ham this song up by acting very confused.
- Don't worry about memorizing the body parts mentioned in the song. Feel free to use whatever comes to mind.

### Picture Book Pairings

Andrews, Sylvia. *Dancing in My Bones.* Illustrated by Ellen Mueller. Harperfestival, 2001. This rhythmic book encourages the listeners to move parts of their body in various means.

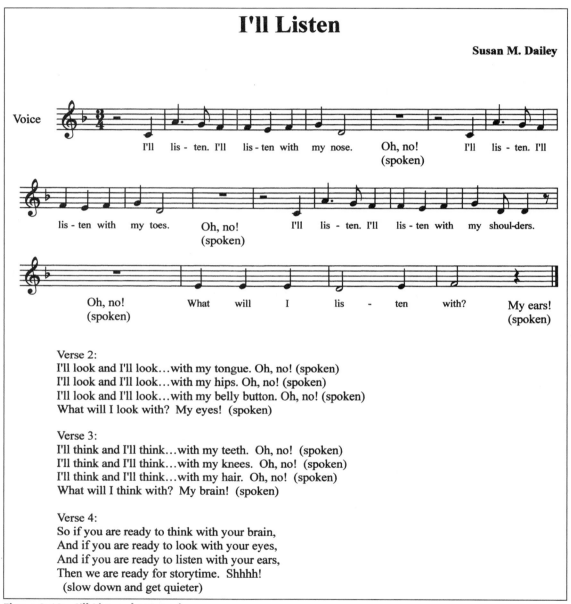

Figure 2-19   I'll Listen sheet music

### 9. I'M SO MAD!

**Words and music by Susan M. Dailey**                                **Feelings**

CD Track 9

Sheet Music, see page 31

**Song Presentation**

You might want to sing along with the CD for this song.
Have the children move as indicated.

**I'm So Mad!**

Verse 1:
I'm so mad! Grrr!
  (*Sing with angry tone to voice, put hands on hips.*)
I'm so mad!
Yes, I am so mad!
Grrr! (*spoken*)

I'm so mad! Grrr!
I'm so mad!
Yes, I am so mad!

I stomp my feet!
  (*Stomp feet.*)
I frown a frown!
  (*Frown.*)
I even yell a yell!
Ahhh! (*Yell.*)

I'm so mad! Grrr!
I'm so mad!
Yes, I am so mad!
Grrr! (*spoken*)

Verse 2:
I'm so glad! Yeah!
  (*Sing with happy tone to voice, pump fist in air.*)
I'm so glad!
Yes, I am so glad!
Yeah! (*spoken*)

I'm so glad! Yeah!
I'm so glad!
Yes, I am so glad!

I clap my hands!
  (*Clap.*)
I smile a smile!
  (*Smile.*)
I even cheer a cheer!
Hurray! (*Shout.*)

I'm so glad! Yeah!
I'm so glad!
Yes, I am so glad!
Yeah! (*spoken*)

## Tips

- You might want to explain to children, especially very young ones, that you are just pretending to be mad.

## Picture Book Pairings

Bang, Molly. ***When Sophie Gets Angry—Really, Really Angry . . .*** Illustrated by author. Blue Sky Press, 1999. A young girl is upset and doesn't know how to manage her anger but takes the time to cool off and regain her composure.

Cabrera, Jane. ***If You're Happy and You Know It***. Illustrated by author. Holiday, 2005. An elephant, a monkey, and a giraffe join other animals to sing different verses of this popular song that encourages everyone to express their happiness through voice and movement.

Palatini, Margie. ***Goldie Is Mad***. Illustrated by author. Hyperion, 2001. A little girl is very upset when her baby brother drools on her doll, but during a time-out, she thinks of some of the things she likes about her brother.

Parr, Todd. ***The Feel Good Book***. Illustrated by author. Little, Brown, 2004. Relates things that make people feel good.

**Figure 2-20  I'm So Mad! sheet music**

## 10. IT'S ALMOST THE HOLIDAYS!

**Words and music by Susan M. Dailey**                    **Christmas, Hanukkah, Kwanzaa**

CD Track 10

Sheet Music, see page 33

## Song Presentation

This is a Quiet Down Activity.

You might want to sing along with the CD for this song.

Have the children wiggle the various body parts as mentioned.

## It's Almost the Holidays!

It's almost the holidays! Don't you know?
It makes me want to wiggle my toe.

It's almost the holidays! Isn't it neat?
It makes me want to wiggle my feet.

It's almost the holidays! Can't you see?
It makes me want to wiggle my knee.

It's almost the holidays, so I hear!
It makes me want to wiggle my rear.

It's almost the holidays! Isn't it grand?
It makes me want to wiggle my hand.

It's almost the holidays, so it's said!
It makes me want to wiggle my head.

But now it's time for a holiday book,
so I'll sit very still and listen and look.
   (*Slow down and get quieter on the last line.*)

## Tips

- Variation

  - You could change "the holidays" to a specific holiday or time of year, e.g. "It's almost summer."
  - You could also sing "It's almost storytime."

## Picture Book Pairings

Ford, Juwanda G. *K Is for Kwanzaa*. Illustrated by Ken Wilson-Max. Scholastic, 1997. Celebrates the African-American holiday Kwanzaa by introducing related words from A to Z, including "Africa," "bendera," "dashiki," and "yams." (Kwanzaa)

Glaser, Linda. *Mrs. Greenberg's Messy Hanukkah*. Illustrated by Nancy Cote. Whitman, 2004. When Rachel makes latkes with her friend Mrs. Greenberg, the project turns out to be a very messy one. (Hanukkah)

Hines, Anna Grossnickle. *Winter Lights: a Season in Poems and Quilts*. Illustrated by author. Greenwillow, 2005. This strikingly illustrated book shares poems celebrating winter, including the holidays. (Holidays)

McKissack, Patricia and Fredrick. *Messy Bessey's Holidays*. Illustrated by Dana Regan. Children's Press, 1999. Bessey and her mother bake cookies for Christmas, Kwanzaa, and Hanukkah, and after cleaning up the kitchen, they distribute the treats to their neighbors. (Christmas, Hanukkah, Kwanzaa)

Wilson, Karma. *Bear Stays Up for Christmas*. Illustrated by Jane Chapman. McElderry, 2004. Bear's friends awaken him the day before Christmas and help him to stay awake as they bake fruitcakes, fill stockings, and sing carols; then, while they sleep, he prepares his own surprise. (Christmas)

**Figure 2-21   It's Almost the Holidays! sheet music**

## 11. I'VE GOT WIGGLES

**Words and music by Susan M. Dailey**                    **Movement, Body**

CD Track 11
Sheet Music, see page 35

### Song Presentation

This is a Quiet Down Activity.

You might want to sing along with the CD for this song.

Have the children wiggle the various body parts mentioned.

### I've Got Wiggles

I've got wiggles inside of me.
They want to come out, as you will see.
Silly wiggles inside of me.

I wiggle my shoulders. I wiggle my toes.
I wiggle my knees and I wiggle my nose.
Still more wiggles inside of me.

I wiggle my fingers. I wiggle my hips.
I wiggle my head and I wiggle my lips.
Still more wiggles inside of me.

I wiggle down low. I wiggle up high,
and now I wave my wiggles good-bye.
No more wiggles inside of me.

### Tips

• To "wiggle my lips," move your finger up and down across them while singing up the musical scale.

### Picture Book Pairings

Cronin, Doreen. *Wiggle*. Illustrated by Scott Menchin. Atheneum, 2005. Rhyming text describes the many ways to wiggle. (Movement)

Hindley, Judy. *Eyes, Nose, Fingers, and Toes*. Illustrated by Brita Granström. Candlewick, 1999. A group of toddlers demonstrate all the fun things that they can do with their eyes, ears, mouths, hands, legs, feet—and everything in between. (Body)

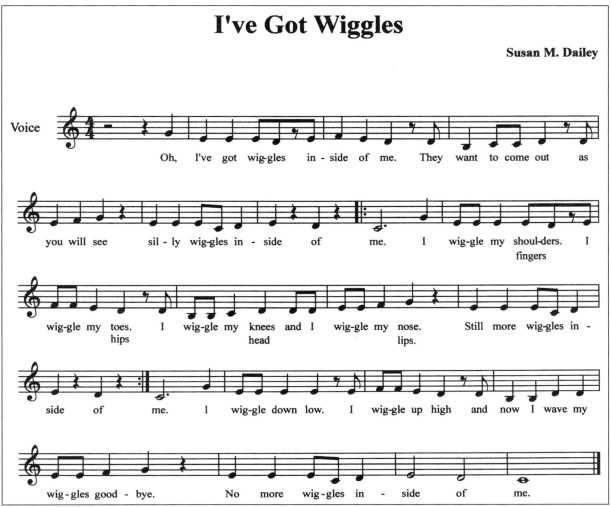

**Figure 2-22 I've Got Wiggles sheet music**

## 12. KITTY CAT, POUNCE

**Words and music by Susan M. Dailey**          **Cats (Animals), Movement**

CD Track 12

Sheet Music, see page 37

### Song Presentation

You might want to sing along with the CD for this song.

Have the children act out the motions as indicated.

Hold out the "and" on the last line.

### Kitty Cat, Pounce

Kitty cat, Kitty cat
   (*Creep fingers.*)

Sneaks out of the house.
Kitty cat, Kitty cat
Creeps up to a mouse,
And . . . pounce!
   (*Make "jumping" motion with fingers.*)

Kitty cat, Kitty cat
   (*Creep fingers.*)
Creeps up to a bird.
Kitty cat, Kitty cat
Is not even heard,
And . . . pounce!
   (*Make "jumping" motion with fingers.*)

But the mouse ran
   (*Make fingers "run."*)
And the bird flew away
   (*Flap hands.*)
So Kitty cat, Kitty cat found
A ball of yarn
   (*Make circle with hands.*)
To play . . . pounce!
   (*Make "jumping" motion with fingers.*)

## Tips

- After singing the song, I brought out a ball of yarn. I held on to the end of yarn and then rolled it back and forth to the kids. The yarn unrolled across the floor, leaving a funny design. If you have adults with the children, you could give each child a small ball of yarn. Have everyone rewind the yarn balls after they've finished.

- Variation

  - You can create visual aids to go along with the song, using the instructions below.

## Picture Book Pairings

Henkes, Kevin. *Kitten's First Full Moon.* Illustrated by author. Greenwillow, 2004. When Kitten mistakes the full moon for a bowl of milk, she ends up tired, wet, and hungry trying to reach it. (Cats)

McDonnell, Flora. *Giddy-Up! Let's Ride!* Illustrated by author. Candlewick, 2002. Describes ways people ride horses and other animals, such as the show jumper on her trrrit-trrroting horse, the raja on his rumpetta-trumping elephant, and the nomad on his lolloppy-plodding camel. (Movement)

Roberts, Bethany. *Cat Skidoo.* Illustrated by R. W. Alley. Holt, 2004. Two active kittens romp outdoors before going back inside for a nap. (Cats)

## Patterns Needed

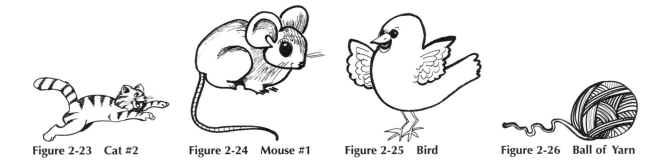

**Figure 2-23   Cat #2**     **Figure 2-24   Mouse #1**     **Figure 2-25   Bird**     **Figure 2-26   Ball of Yarn**

## Visual Aid Creation

- See above patterns / CD files 2-23 through 2-26. Download and print .pdf files or photocopy them.
- Color the pieces.
- Attach craft sticks to the pieces. Use with the lap stage from "Joey Goes Fishing" story.

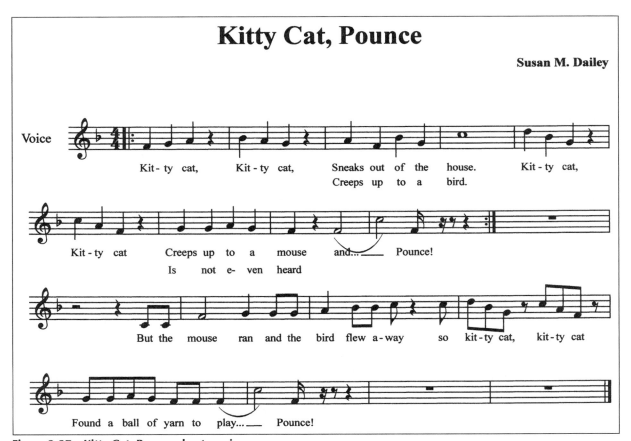

**Figure 2-27   Kitty Cat, Pounce sheet music**

## 13. LITTLE CHICKS

**Words and music by Susan M. Dailey**                    **Chickens (Birds), Farms, Babies**

CD Track 13

Sheet Music, see page 40

### Song Presentation

Create the visual aid using the patterns on page 39.

Have the children move as indicated.

You might want to sing along with the CD for this song.

### Little Chicks

Tiptoe to the henhouse.
   (*Creep fingers.*)
Peek in the door.
   (*Put hand above eyes and look around.*)
See the little eggs,
one, two, three, four.
   (*Hold up fingers while counting.*)

But when will they hatch?
   (*Hold out hands in questioning gesture.*)
When will they appear?
Listen! Listen
   (*Cup hand around ear.*)
and you will hear . . .

Peck, peck, peck
   (*Pinch thumb and index finger together, make up and down motion.*)
And pick, pick, pick
And out of an egg
   (*Cup hands, then open them up.*)
comes one little chick!

(*Repeat 3rd stanza 2 more times. Then sing:*)

Peck, peck, peck
and pick, pick, pick
and peck, peck, peck
and pick, pick, pick
and out of the egg
comes the last little chick!

### Tips

- Variation

  - You can create visual aids for each of the children.

### Picture Book Pairings

Rathmann, Peggy. *The Day the Babies Crawled Away.* Illustrated by author. Putnam's, 2003. A boy follows fives babies who crawl away from a picnic and saves the day by bringing them back. (Babies)

Shannon, George. *Tippy-Toe Chick, Go.* Illustrated by Laura Dronzek. Greenwillow, 2003. When a mean dog blocks the path to the garden where a delicious breakfast awaits, Little Chick shows her family how brave and clever she is. (Chickens)

Williams, Linda. *Horse in the Pigpen.* Illustrated by Megan Lloyd. HarperCollins, 2002. A child tries to get his mother's attention as chaos erupts around the family farm. (Farms)

### Patterns Needed

Figure 2-28   Little Chicks photo

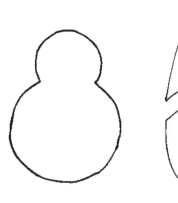

Figure 2-29   Chick and Egg Patterns

### Visual Aid Creation

1. See pattern above / CD file 2-29. Download and print .pdf files or photocopy them.
2. Using the patterns provided, cut four eggs from white construction paper or tagboard.
3. Punch holes in each egg piece.
4. Use a paper fastener to attach the two pieces of the egg to each other.
5. Cut four chicks from yellow construction paper.
6. Cut small orange triangles for the beaks.
7. I used 1/4 inch blue dots for the eyes, but you could easily make eyes by using a hole punch.
8. Assemble the chicks.
9. I attached each egg to a paint stirrer.

**Figure 2-30   Little Chicks sheet music**

## 14. MY MONSTER

**Words and music by Susan M. Dailey**                    **Monsters**

CD Track 14

Sheet Music, see page 43

### Song Presentation

Make the visual aid using the pattern provided on page 42.

You might want to sing along with the CD for this song.

Sing a line and have the children repeat it.

Have the children point to the various body parts as you sing about them.

Make three kissing noises during the chorus.

### My Monster

Verse 1:
He has big feet
With curly toes
And on his face
A yellow nose.

Chorus:
He's my adorable,
Huggable, kissable
(kiss, kiss, kiss) monster!

Verse 2:
His legs are short.
The left one's blue.
The right one's green
And purple, too.
(Chorus)

Verse 3:
His body's long
And rather wide.
He has two arms
On either side.
(Chorus)

Verse 4:
He has small ears.
He has big eyes,
But his smile

Is supersize.
(Chorus)

## Tips

- Variation

    - You can create a visual aid to go along with the song, using the instructions below.

## Picture Book Pairings

Sendak, Maurice. *Where the Wild Things Are.* Illustrated by author. Harper & Row, 1963. A naughty little boy, sent to bed without his supper, sails to the land of the wild things where he becomes their king.

Willems, Mo. *Your Pal Mo Willems Presents Leonardo the Terrible Monster.* Illustrated by author. Hyperion, 2005. Leonardo is a terrible monster—he can't seem to frighten anyone. When he discovers the perfect nervous little boy, will he scare the lunch out of him? Or will he think of something better?

## Patterns Needed

**Figure 2-31    Monster**

## Visual Aid Creation

1. See pattern above / CD file 2-31. Download and print the .pdf file or photocopy it.
2. Color the pattern, as indicated in the song.

**Figure 2-32 My Monster sheet music**

## 15. OH, I SEE A BUTTERFLY

**Words and music by Susan M. Dailey**                    **Butterflies (Bugs)**

CD Track 15

Sheet Music, see page 45

### Song Presentation

Fashion a butterfly for each child by enlarging the pattern on page 45.

Have the children move their butterflies as indicated.

You might want to sing along with the CD for this song.

### Oh, I See a Butterfly

Oh, I see a butterfly,
way up high in the sky
butterfly.

Flying, flying all around,
Landing gently on the ground
butterfly.

Flying high and flying low,
flying fast and flying slow
butterfly.

Landed on my hand and nose,
on my tummy, on my toes
Butterfly, butterfly, butterfly.

### Tips

- Have the children hold their butterfly by pinching the "body" part. When they move it up and down, it will appear to flap its wings.
- You could have the children decorate the butterflies for a craft. One way to decorate them would be to have the children paint on one side of the butterfly. Then fold the other wing over and rub. This will create a mirror image on the butterfly's wings.
- In 2001, Weston Woods produced a wonderful video of *Waiting for Wings* with the words set to music.

### Picture Book Pairings

Carle, Eric. *The Very Hungry Caterpillar*. Illustrated by author. Philomel, 1987. Follows the progress of a hungry little caterpillar as he eats his way through a varied and very large quantity of food until, full at last, he forms a cocoon around himself and goes to sleep.

Ehlert, Lois. *Waiting for Wings*. Illustrated by author. Harcourt, 2001. The life cycle of the butterfly is simply told in this rhyming tale.

### Pattern Needed

- See Figure 2-33

### Visual Aid Creation

1. See pattern / CD file 2-33 for the pattern. Download and print the .pdf file or photocopy it.
2. Trace the pattern on construction paper.
3. Glue or tape strips of black construction paper in the folded area to create antennae. You can roll the ends of the paper around a pencil to curl them. You could also use chenille sticks for the antennae.
4. Staple along the folded line.

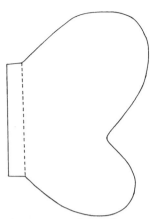

Figure 2-33   Butterfly

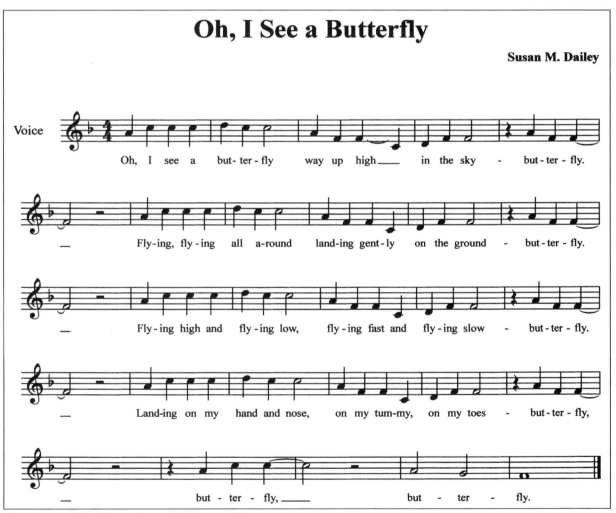

Figure 2-34   Oh, I See a Butterfly sheet music

## 16. PICNIC

**Words and music by Susan M. Dailey**                    **Picnics, Food, Summer**

CD Track 16

Sheet Music, see page 49

### Song Presentation

Make picnic baskets for the children using the patterns provided on pages 47-48.

Have the children start with all the food lying in front of them. As you sing about a certain food, have them put it in their basket.

Learn the song by listening to the CD or by playing the sheet music.

Pause between the items mentioned in the last verse so the children can put the items into their baskets.

### Picnic

Chorus:
P-I-C-N-I-C,
Picnic time, yes, sir-ree!

Verse 1:
Pack a basket with lots of stuff!
Lemonade, is that enough? No! (*spoken*)
Hot dogs, hot dogs, is that enough? No! (*spoken*)
Pretzels, pretzels, is that enough? No! (*spoken*)

*Repeat chorus.*

Verse 2:
Pack a basket with even more stuff!
Watermelon, is that enough? No! (*spoken*)
Apples, apples, is that enough? No! (*spoken*)
Cookies, cookies, is that enough? No! (*spoken*)

*Repeat chorus.*

Verse 3:
Pack some cupcakes, a lollipop to lick
A Frisbee® and a ball to kick
Is that enough? Yes! (*spoken*)

## Tips

- Variations
    - You could make a large picnic basket for yourself. Give each child a picture of food. Have each children put food in the basket as you sing about it.
    - You could eliminate the basket and just have the children put their pieces on the magnetic/flannel board.
    - You could have the children put their food into a real picnic basket.
    - You could get plastic food.

## Picture Book Pairings

Dodds, Dayle Ann. *Minnie's Diner.* Illustrated by John Manders. Candlewick, 2004. Rhyming tale of five boys and their father who forget about their chores on the farm to enjoy Minnie's good cooking, each requesting double what the previous one ordered. (Food)

Helldorfer, Mary-Claire. *Got to Dance.* Illustrated by Hiroe Nakata. Doubleday, 2004. A young city girl dances away the summertime blues with her grandfather. (Summer)

Kasza, Keiko. *Pig's Picnic.* Illustrated by author. Putnam, 1988. Mr. Pig, on his way to call on Miss Pig, allows his animal friends to persuade him to don various handsome portions of their own bodies, with an alarming result. (Picnics)

## Patterns Needed

**Figure 2-35    Picnic Basket photo**

**Figure 2-36    Picnic Basket diagram**

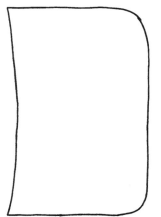

**Figure 2-37    Picnic Basket sample**

**Figure 2-38    Lemonade**

**Figure 2-39 Lollipop**

**Figure 2-40 Soccer Ball**

**Figure 2-41 Frisbee®**

### Visual Aid Creation

To make the picnic basket, you need the following materials:

Brown construction paper

Strips of tan paper

Chenille sticks (pipe cleaners)

1. Trace and cut out the shape of the basket on construction paper. Make two pieces.
2. Make slits in both basket pieces. Leave approximately a one-inch margin on top, bottom and outside. (see Figure 2-36)
3. Weave the tan strips through both sides of the basket. Glue down strips at top and bottom. Trim excess strips. (see Figure 2-37)
4. Staple the edges of the baskets together.
5. Punch one hole in either side of basket along the top.
6. Put a chenille stick through each hole. If you're making a large basket, you will need to use two chenille sticks and twist them together.
7. See pages 47-48 / CD files 2-38 through 2-41. Download and print .pdf files or photocopy them.
8. Use the patterns for hot dog, pretzel, watermelon, apple, cookie, and cupcake from "Aiken Drum" on page 138–140.
9. Color the patterns provided.
10. You might want to laminate the picnic items. If you want to protect the basket, you can cover it with clear Con-tact® paper.

# Picnic

Susan M. Dailey

Figure 2-42  Picnic sheet music

## 17. PLAYING WITH MY PARENTS

**Words and music by Susan M. Dailey**                    **Toys/Playing, Parents (Families)**

CD Track 17
Sheet Music, see page 51

### Song Presentation

You might want to sing along with the CD for this song.

Have the children stand and act out the motions as indicated.

### Playing with My Parents

My mom and I play golf.
  (*Pretend to putt golf ball.*)
My dad and I go biking.
  (*Roll hands around each other.*)
My mom and I go swimming.
  (*Make swimming motions.*)
My dad and I go hiking.
  (*Pump arms back and forth.*)

My mom and I play tennis.
  (*Pretend to throw ball up and then serve it.*)
My dad and I play baseball.
  (*Pretend to hit ball.*)
But we all, yes, we all
  (*Nod head.*)
love . . . basketball!
  (*Pretend to dribble ball, then shoot it.*)

### Tips

- At the end when we pretended to shoot, I'd ask a few kids if they made their shot. They really enjoyed the pretending aspect.

### Picture Book Pairings

Heap, Sue. *What Shall We Play?* Illustrated by author. Candlewick, 2002. Lily May and her friends have fun pretending to be trees, cars, cats, Jell-O®, and fairies. (Toys/Playing)

Wells, Rosemary. *Noisy Nora.* Illustrated by author. Dial, 1997. Feeling neglected, Nora makes more and more noise to attract her parents' attention. (Family)

**Figure 2-43   Playing with My Parents sheet music**

## 18. POPCORN

**Words and music by Susan M. Dailey**                                    **Food**

CD Track 18

Sheet Music, see page 53

### Song Presentation

Learn the song by listening to the CD or by playing the sheet music.

Sing a line and have the children repeat it.

Have the children move as indicated.

### Popcorn

Open the door.
  (*Pretend to pull.*)
Put the bag in.
  (*Lay one hand out, palm up.*)
Then push the button.
  (*Pretend to push.*)
Watch it spin.
  (*Move finger in circle.*)

Listen and soon
  (*Put hand to ear.*)
You'll hear a pop.
  (*Clap hands on pop.*)
Pop . . .
  (*Say "pop" many times, getting closer together just before saying "stop."*)
. . . pop, stop!
  (*Hold up one hand, palm out.*)

Smells so delicious
  (*Sniff air.*)
Yummy to eat
  (*Pretend to put kernels in mouth, gulp.*)
Say, do you know
  (*Point to kids.*)
This tasty treat?
  (*Rub stomach.*)

It's popcorn! (*spoken*)

## Tips

- You can have the pop section go on as long as you'd like.
- Sing a rhythmic pattern and have the children repeat it.

## Picture Book Pairings

Seeger, Pete and Paul DuBois Jacobs. ***Some Friends to Feed: the Story of Stone Soup.*** Illustrated by Michael Hays. Putnam, 2005. A poor but clever traveler finds a way to get the townspeople to share their food with him in this retelling of a classic tale, set in Germany at the end of the Thirty Years War.

# Popcorn

Susan M. Dailey

**Figure 2-44  Popcorn sheet music**

## 19. RAINBOW FARM

**Words and music by Susan M. Dailey** **Farms, Colors**

CD Track 19
Sheet Music, see page 56

### Song Presentation

Make visual aids using the patterns provided on page 55.
Put the patterns on the board as you sing the song and let the children identify the colors.

### Rainbow Farm

I live on a rainbow farm.
I see yellow, red and blue,
black and white, orange and brown,
green, pink and purple, too.

There's a chick that is yellow,
a barn that is red,
a pig that is pink
from tail to head.

There's a tractor that is green,
a cow that is brown,
Blue and purple flowers
grow all around.

There's a pumpkin that is orange,
a sheep that is white,
a big black cat
that's dark as night.

I live on a rainbow farm
with lots of colors that I see.
Rainbow farm, rainbow farm,
best place on earth for me!

### Tips

- For a craft activity, I gave each of the children a booklet with the words. They glued the appropriate picture on each page.

## Picture Book Pairings

Shannon, George. *White Is for Blueberry.* Illustrated by Laura Dronzek. Greenwillow, 2005. Encourages the reader to look at objects in nature from another perspective, observing their colors in a new way. (Colors)

Spurr, Elizabeth. *Farm Life.* Illustrated by Steve Björkman. Holiday House, 2003. Rhymed descriptions of life on a farm introduce basic colors and the numbers one to ten. (Farms)

## Patterns Needed

**Figure 2-45   Chick**

**Figure 2-46   Barn**

**Figure 2-47   Pig**

**Figure 2-48   Tractor**

**Figure 2-49   Flower #2**

**Figure 2-50   Flower #3**

**Figure 2-51   Pumpkin**

**Figure 2-52   Sheep #2**

**Figure 2-53   Cat #3**

**Visual Aid Creation**

1. See page 55 / CD files 2-45 through 2-53 for the pattern. Download and print .pdf files or photocopy them.
2. Use the cow from "Down on Grandpa's Farm" on page 149.
3. Color the patterns or copy them on construction paper in the appropriate colors.

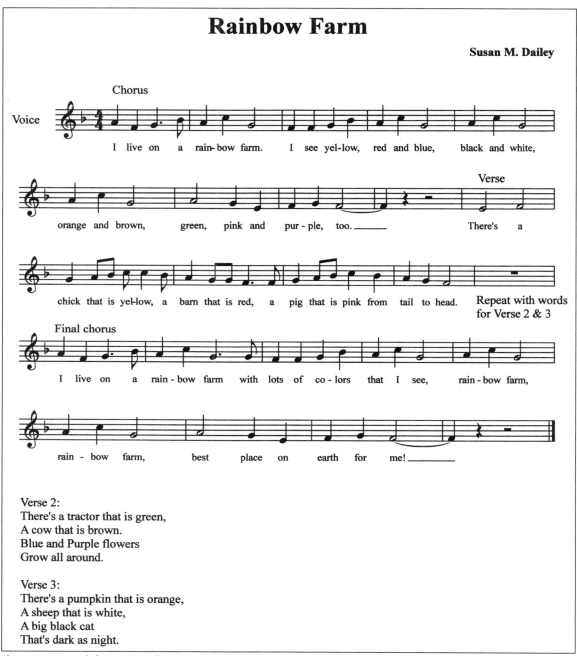

**Figure 2-54   Rainbow Farm sheet music**

## 20. ROLL THE SNOW

**Words and music by Susan M. Dailey**                                    **Winter**

CD Track 20

Sheet Music, see page 58

### Song Presentation

This is a Name Tag Activity.

Make name tags for each child using the pattern below.

Learn the song by listening to the CD or by playing the sheet music.

Have the children act out the words as indicated.

As you sing the song, have a few of the children bring their name tags to the magnetic/flannel board.

Count the number on the board. Sing the song again, filling in the correct number. I sang sample verses on the CD.

### Roll the Snow

Roll the snow.
  (*Roll hands.*)
See it grow.
  (*Roll hands farther apart.*)
Add two eyes and a hat just so.
  (*Point to eyes and top of head.*)
Oh, what fun!
Now it's done.
One snowman in the winter sun.
  (*Hold up one finger.*)
Who will add another one?

### Picture Book Pairings

Stojic, Manya. *Snow.* Illustrated by author. Random House, 2002. As snow approaches and begins to fall, Moose, Bear, Fox, and other forest creatures prepare for winter.

### Patterns Needed

• See Figure 2-55

### Visual Aid Creation

1. See pattern / CD file 2-55. Download and print the .pdf file or photocopy it.

**Figure 2-55   Snowman**

2. Color the pattern.
3. Put magnets on the back.

Figure 2-56   **Roll the Snow sheet music**

## 21. SEARCHING FOR MY CLOTHES

**Words and music by Susan M. Dailey**                                        **Clothes**

CD Track 21
Sheet Music, see page 61

### Song Presentation

You might want to sing along with the CD for this song.

Have the children do the motions as indicated.

### Searching for My Clothes

Verse 1:
It's time to go!
  (*Tap wrist.*)
It's time to go!
Where are my socks?
  (*Hold hands out in questioning motion.*)
I don't know!
(*Shake head.*)

I searched high and I searched low.
  (*Put hand above eyes, look upward, then downward.*)
Where are my socks?
I don't know!

I searched by the computer
  (*Pretend to type on keyboard.*)
and by the rocking chair.
  (*Pretend to rock.*)
I finally looked in the toy box.
  (*Pretend to lift lid.*)
What are they doing there?
  (*Shrug shoulders.*)

I pulled them on,
  (*Pretend to put on.*)
found a hole in the toe.
So who cares?
  (*Shrug shoulders.*)
I'm ready to go.
  (*Nod head.*)

You mean I have to wear shoes? (*spoken*)

Verse 2:
It's time to go!
  (*Tap wrist.*)
It's time to go!
Where are my shoes?
  (*Hold hands out in questioning motion.*)
I don't know!
  (*Shake head.*)

I searched high and I searched low.
  (*Put hand above eyes, look upward, then downward.*)
Where are my shoes?
I don't know!

I searched by the computer
  (*Pretend to type on keyboard.*)
and by the rocking chair.
  (*Pretend to rock.*)
I finally looked in the freezer.
  (*Pretend to open door.*)
What are they doing there?
  (*Shrug shoulders.*)

I put them on.
  (*Pretend to put on.*)
Tied the laces in a bow.
  (*Pretend to tie.*)
My shoes are on

I'm ready to go.
  (*Nod head.*)

You mean I have to wear a coat? (*spoken*)

Verse 3:
It's time to go!
  (*Tap wrist.*)
It's time to go!
Where is my coat?
  (*Hold hands out in questioning motion.*)
I don't know!
  (*Shake head.*)

I searched high and I searched low.
  (*Put hand above eyes, look upward, then downward.*)
Where is my coat?
I don't know!

I searched by the computer
  (*Pretend to type on keyboard.*)
and by the rocking chair.
  (*Pretend to rock.*)
I finally looked in the closet.
  (*Pretend to open door.*)
What is it doing there?
  (*Shrug shoulders.*)

I put it on,
  (*Pretend to put on.*)
zipped it up just so.
  (*Pretend to tie.*)
I'm finally ready.
Come on, let's go!
  (*Nod head.*)

## Tips

• If you're doing a program about a specific type of clothing, e.g. shoes, you might want to just sing that verse.

## Picture Book Pairings

Dodds, Dayle Ann. ***The Kettles Get New Clothes.*** Illustrated by Jill McElmurry. Candlewick, 2002. When the small town store where they usually buy their clothes changes hands, the Kettles are in for a surprise on their annual shopping trip.

**Figure 2-57  Searching for My Clothes sheet music**

## 22. SOMETHING'S HIDING IN A FLOWER

**Words and music by Susan M. Dailey**                          **Flowers, Bugs, Summer**

CD Track 22

Sheet Music, see page 65

### Song Presentation

Make the visual aid using the patterns provided on pages 63-64.

As you sing the third line of each verse, reveal what's hiding in the appropriate color by lifting the flap in the middle size flower.

You might want to sing along with the CD for this song.

### Something's Hiding in a Flower

Something's hiding in a flower.
Come on, let's go see.
Open up the red flower.
Look, it's a bumblebee!

Something's hiding in a flower,
giving it a hug.
Open up the yellow flower.
Look, it's a ladybug!

Something's hiding in a flower.
Can you guess? I can't!
Open up the purple flower.
Look, it's an ant!

Something's hiding in a flower,
making the flower squirm.
Open up the blue flower.
Look, it's a worm!

Something's hiding in a flower,
feeling rather shy.
Open up the orange flower.
Look, it's a butterfly!

Something's hiding in a flower.
It is a big surprise!
Open up the pink flower.
I can't believe my eyes!
It's a . . .

### Tips

• You can change what's hiding in the pink flower if you sing the song several times.

### Picture Book Pairings

Ashman, Linda. *To the Beach.* Illustrated by Nadine Bernard Westcott. Harcourt, 2005. A family keeps forgetting the things they need to take to the beach. (Summer)

Ehlert, Lois. *Planting a Rainbow.* Illustrated by author. Harcourt, 1988. A mother and child plant a rainbow of flowers in the family garden. (Flowers)

Ward, Jennifer. *Over in the Garden.* Illustrations by Kenneth J. Spengler. Rising Moon, 2002. Over in the garden, mother insects and their children enjoy various activities from morning sun to evening moon. (Bugs)

## Patterns Needed

Figure 2-58   Flower Board photo #1

Figure 2-59   Flower Board photo #2

Figure 2-61   Flower Pattern Medium

Figure 2-62   Flower Pattern Large

Figure 2-60   Flower Pattern Small

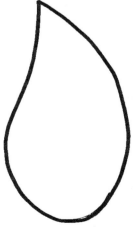

Figure 2-63   Leaf #2

Figure 2-64   Ant

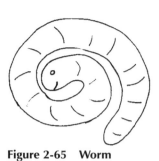

Figure 2-65    Worm

Figure 2-66    Baby

Figure 2-67    Elephant #1

Figure 2-68    Clown

Figure 2-69    Birthday Cake

Figure 2-70    Fish #2

## Visual Aid Creation

1. See page 63 and above / CD files 2-60 through 2-70. Download and print .pdf files or photocopy them.
2. Use the bumblebee, ladybug and butterfly from "Do You Have a Ladybug?" on page 99.
3. Trace the three sizes of flowers on red, yellow, purple, blue, orange and pink construction paper. Fold the petals so they stand up.
4. Attach the medium size flowers to the matching large ones with a staple. Place the staple at the top of the medium flower so you can lift it like a flap to show what's underneath.
5. Glue the small flower on top of the medium one.
6. Now glue the six flowers on foam core board or illustration board.
7. Add stems. Enlarge and trace the leaf patterns on green construction paper or make your own leaves.
8. Photocopy and color the other graphics.
9. Glue the bumblebee, ladybug, ant, worm and butterfly into the center of the large flower of the appropriate color. Make sure the other flower layers will cover it.
10. I didn't glue anything into the pink one because I changed it each week during the session. Several objects are provided for this purpose. I used an Artwaxer®, a machine which puts thin stripes of wax on the back of an object. However, you could use Velcro® or double-stick tape to put the "surprise" inside this flower.

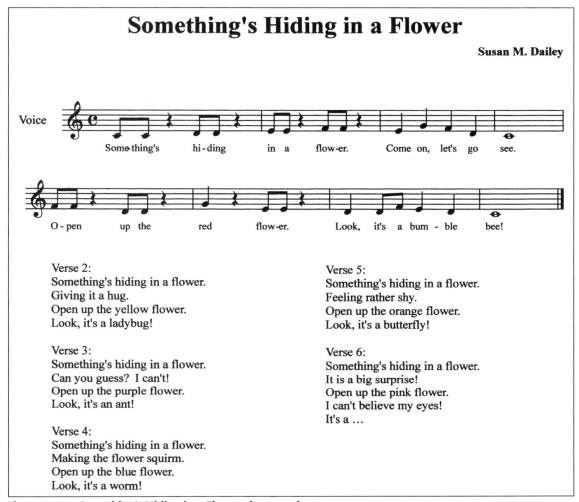

**Figure 2-71** Something's Hiding in a Flower sheet music

## 23. SPRING FLOWERS

**Words and music by Susan M. Dailey**                                    **Spring, Flowers, Colors**

CD Track 23

Sheet Music, see page 67

### Song Presentation

This is a Name Tag Activity.

Make name tags for each child using the flower patterns from "Earth Song" on page 102 or from "Something's Hiding in a Flower" on page 63.

Learn the song by listening to the CD or by playing the sheet music.

Have the children move as indicated.

As you sing the song, have the children bring their name tags to the magnetic/flannel board at the end of the appropriate verse.

### Spring Flowers

It is spring!
Let's plant some seeds.
  (*Hold out one hand, palm up, pretend to plant seeds in it.*)
Here come the sun
  (*Make circle with hands above head.*)
and rain they need.
  (*Flutter fingers downward.*)
Wait awhile
and they will grow
  (*Bring hands upward.*)
Pretty blue flowers
in a row.

(*Repeat with pink and white flowers.*)

### Picture Book Pairings

Bentley, Dawn. ***Good Night, Sweet Butterflies***. Illustrated by Heather Cahoon. Little Simon, 2003. Young ones will love learning to count backwards from nine to one as touchable, colorful butterflies disappear one by one as bedtime approaches. (Colors)

Bunting, Eve. ***Flower Garden***. Illustrated by Kathryn Hewitt. Harcourt, 1994. Helped by her father, a young girl prepares a flower garden as a birthday surprise for her mother. (Flowers)

Thompson, Lauren. ***Mouse's First Spring***. Illustrated by Buket Erdogan. Simon & Schuster, 2005. A mouse and its mother experience the delights of nature on a windy spring day. (Spring)

### Patterns Needed

• Flowers

### Visual Aid Creation

1. See pages 63 and 102 / CD file 2-60 or 3-13. Download and print .pdf files or photocopy them.
2. Trace the patterns on blue, white, and pink construction paper.
3. Put magnets on the back.

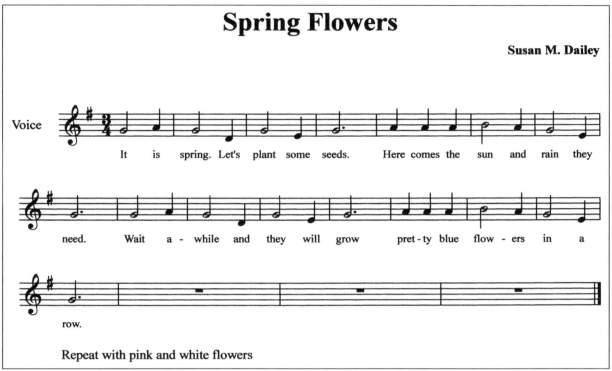

**Spring Flowers**

Susan M. Dailey

It is spring. Let's plant some seeds. Here comes the sun and rain they
need. Wait a - while and they will grow pret - ty blue flow - ers in a
row.

Repeat with pink and white flowers

**Figure 2-72   Spring Flowers sheet music**

## 24. STAND UP

**Words and music by Susan M. Dailey**

CD Track 24

Sheet Music, see page 68

### Song Presentation

This is a Closing Song.

You might want to sing along with the CD for this song.

Have the children move as indicated.

### Stand Up

Stand up! Reach up high.
Now it's time to wave good-bye.

Tap your toes. Slap your thighs.
Now it's time to wave good-bye.

Click your tongue. Sigh a sigh.
Now it's time to wave good-bye.

But come back soon or I will cry.
Now it's time to wave good-bye.

## Tips

• Cry very melodramatically on the second to last line.

**Figure 2-73   Stand Up sheet music**

## 25. STRANGE THING HAPPENED TO ME

**Words and music by Susan M. Dailey**                    **Movement, Nonsense**

CD Track 25

Sheet Music, see page 70

### Song Presentation

This is a Stretch where the children have a chance to move around between stories.

You might want to sing along with the CD for this song.

Have the children move as indicated.

**Strange Thing Happened to Me**

Verse 1:
Mom, I know I'm late,
But I really shouldn't be.
I started out on time,
but a strange thing happened to me!

I was walking home
when all of a sudden
my legs began to shake.

They went shake, shake, shake,
shake, shake, shake,
shake, shake, shake, shake,
shake, shake, shake,
shake, shake, shake,
shake, shake, shake, shake,
so I had to get down on the ground!

(*Repeat with "hop" for verse 2. Repeat with "spin" for verse 3, but change last line to:*)

But I finally got home and I'm late and I'm tired and I have to sit down on the ground.

## Tips

• I just knelt on the ground at the end of verses 1 and 2, but you could sit down.

## Picture Book Pairings

George, Kristine O'Connell. *Up!* Illustrated by Hiroe Nakata. Clarion, 2005. Rhyming text and illustrations animate the feeling of "up" as experienced by a little girl with her father. (Movement)

Wood, Audrey. *Silly Sally.* Illustrated by author. Harcourt, 1992. A rhyming story of Silly Sally, who makes many friends as she travels to town—backward and upside down. (Nonsense)

Figure 2-74   Strange Thing Happened to Me sheet music

## 26. THREE FROGS ON A LOG

**Words and music by Susan M. Dailey**                    **Frogs, Counting**

CD Track 26

Sheet Music, see page 73

### Song Presentation

Make the visual aid using the instructions below and the pattern provided on page 73.
Learn the song by listening to the CD or by playing the sheet music.

### Three Frogs on a Log

Three frogs on a log,
one fly in the sky:
Buzzzzzzzz.

The one fly flew nearby
those three frogs on a log.
Then, zip, zap, gulp!
Splash! (*spoken*)

(*Repeat with two, then one.*)

### Tips

- When you are singing the song, hold the fishing line loop and move the fly around the frogs.
- When you sing "zip, zap," push the chenille stick out through the frog's mouth and hook the fishing line loop.
- Squeeze the sides of the mouth with one hand so they open. Pull the chenille stick back inside with the other hand when you sing "gulp."
- Then make the frog "splash" off the board.
- Variation

    - You could do this without the prop.
    - On the first line, hold up the proper number of fingers on each verse.
    - Move your finger around for the fly on the third line.
    - Make a frog's mouth by placing your palms together. Raise the top hand keeping your wrists together. Bring the top hand down quickly on "gulp."

### Picture Book Pairings

Cowley, Joy. ***Red-Eyed Tree Frog.*** Illustrated by Nic Bishop. Scholastic, 1999. This frog found in the rain forest of Central America spends the night searching for food while also being careful not to become dinner for some other animal. (Frogs)

Wood, Audrey. *Ten Little Fish.* Illustrated by Bruce Wood. Blue Sky Press, 2004. Ten little fish swim along an ocean reef, each finding a different reason to leave until there is only one left. (Counting)

Figure 2-75    Frog photo #1

Figure 2-76    Frog photo #2

### Patterns Needed

• Frog body / CD file 2-81

### Visual Aid Creation

To make the prop, you need the following materials:

Green plastic canvas-7 count

Green yarn

6 frog eyes

3 red chenille sticks

Green craft foam sheets

3 paint stirrers

Styrofoam board-approximately 20" x 12" and at least 1" thick

Brown or black foam sheet

Black yarn

Fishing line

Figure 2-77    Frog example #1

1. To make one frog head, cut **three** pieces of plastic canvas into 20-hole squares.
2. Turn the squares so they look like diamonds. Cut a 7-hole triangle from each point to make hexagons and throw triangles away. (*See example 1.*)
3. Lay **two** hexagons on top of each other. Whipstitch sides A, B, and C of the two hexagons together (*See examples 2 and 3.*) I used white yarn for demonstration purposes. You should use green.

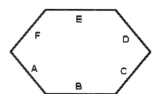

Figure 2-78    Frog example #2

Figure 2-79    Frog example #3

4. Stitch side D of the top hexagon **only** to side F of the third hexagon. (*See example 4.*)
5. Stitch side E of the third hexagon to side E of the top hexagon.
6. Continue by stitching side D of the third hexagon to side F of the top hexagon. When you are finished, the "mouth" will open when you squeeze on the sides.

**Figure 2-80    Frog example #4**

7. Push the shanks of the frog eyes in place. You will probably have to cut a small hole to do this.
8. Cut a small hole in the back to allow a chenille stick to go through. This is the frog's "tongue."
9. Fasten the frog's head to the paint stirrer with yarn or wire.
10. Use the pattern to make the frog's body out of craft foam. You might need to enlarge or reduce it depending on the size of the head. Glue it to the paint stirrer.
11. Make two more frogs.
12. Push the paint stirrers into the Styrofoam board.
13. Roll the brown or black foam sheet into a tube. Pin it to the Styrofoam board in front of the frogs for the log. Color the space in front of the log blue to represent water.
14. To make the flies, wrap some black yarn into a loop and tie the loop in the middle. Attach a loop of fishing line to the fly.

**Figure 2-81    Frog Body Pattern**

Figure 2-82    Three Frogs on a Log sheet music

## 27. TURKEY CHEER

**Words and music by Susan M. Dailey** **Thanksgiving**

CD Track 27

Sheet Music, see page 75

### Song Presentation

This is a Name Tag Activity.

Make name tags for each child using the pattern below.

Learn the song by listening to the CD or by playing the sheet music.

As you sing the song, at the end of the appropriate verse, have the children bring their name tags to the magnetic/flannel board.

Count the number on the board. Sing the song again filling in the correct number. I sang sample verses on the CD.

### Turkey Cheer

One little turkey did appear
when Thanksgiving was very near.
But we need more turkeys here.
Then we'll give a turkey cheer.
Gobble, gobble, gobble, gobble, gobble!

### Picture Book Pairings

Greene, Rhonda Gowler. *The Very First Thanksgiving Day.* Illustrated by Susan Graber. Atheneum, 2002. Rhyming verses trace the events leading up to the first Thanksgiving Day.

Levine, Abby. *This Is the Turkey.* Illustrated by Paige Billin-Frye. Whitman, 2000. Describes in rhyme the activities of a young boy and his extended family as they share a special Thanksgiving.

### Visual Aid Creation

1. See pattern / CD file 2-83. Download and print the .pdf file or photocopy it.
2. Color the pattern to make the pieces.
3. Put magnets on the back.

**Figure 2-83   Turkey**

# Turkey Cheer

Susan M. Dailey

**Figure 2-84  Turkey Cheer sheet music**

## 28. U.S.A.

**Words and music by Susan M. Dailey**                    **Fourth of July, America, Summer**

CD Track 28

Sheet Music, see page 77

### Song Presentation

Make up pieces using the pattern on page 76.

Give each child a U.S.A. card.

When you sing the chorus, have the children hold up their cards on the second and fourth lines.

Get an American flag or find a picture of it.

When you sing the verses, point to the appropriate area on the flag.

You might want to sing along with the CD for this song.

### U.S.A.

Chorus:

Where do you live?
The U.S.A.
What did you say?
The U.S.A.

What are the colors on the flag?
Red, white, blue.

(*Repeat chorus.*)

What do you see on the flag?
Stars and stripes.
(*Final chorus.*)

### Tips

- Explain what U.S.A. stands for.
- Variation

    - Instead of having a flag, have red, blue and white cards for the first verse and one
      card with stars and another with stripes for the second verse.

### Picture Book Pairings

Bates, Katherine Lee. *America the Beautiful.* Illustrated by Chris Gall. Little, Brown, 2004. Four verses
    of the nineteenth-century poem, illustrated by the author's great-great-grandnephew. (America)
Thompson, Lauren. *Mouse's First Summer*. Illustrated by Buket Erdogan. Simon & Schuster, 2004.
    (Fourth of July, Summer) Mouse and Minka experience the colors of summer as they explore a pic-
    nic, which ends with fireworks.

### Pattern Needed

**Figure 2-85   U.S.A. card**

### Visual Aid Creation

1. See pattern above / CD file 2-85 for the pattern. Download and print the .pdf file or photocopy it.
2. Color the letters if you'd like.

**Figure 2-86** U.S.A. sheet music

## 29. WE CAN

**Words and music by Susan M. Dailey**                          **Movement**

CD Track 29

Sheet Music, see page 79

### Song Presentation

This is a Quiet Down Activity.

You might want to sing along with the CD for this song.

Have the children move as indicated.

### We Can

We can swing our arms.
We can reach to the skies.

We can nod our heads
and we can blink our two eyes.

We can bend down low.
We can stretch our arms wide.
We can wiggle our fingers
and shake our head side to side.

We can tap our knees.
We can shake our hips.
We can shrug our shoulders.
We can smack our lips.
We can sing la, la, la, la, la, la, la, la, la, la, la.

We can wiggle our toes.
We can wrinkle our nose.
We can make our hands clap,
and lay them down in our lap.

## Picture Book Pairings

Davis, Katie. *Who Hops?* Illustrated by author. Harcourt, 1998. Lists creatures that hop, fly, slither, swim, and crawl, as well as some others that don't.

Hindley, Judy. *Can You Move like an Elephant?* Illustrated by Manya Stojic. Barrons Educational Series, 2003. Animals move in many ways and the reader is asked to move in the same way.

# We Can

**Susan M. Dailey**

**Figure 2-87 We Can sheet music**

## 30. WHAT GROWS IN MY GARDEN?

**Words and music by Susan M. Dailey**                              **Gardens, Food, Summer**

CD Track 30

Sheet Music, see page 81

### Song Presentation

This is a Name Tag Activity.

Make a name tag for each child using the patterns on page 81.

Learn the song by listening to the CD or by playing the sheet music.

As you sing the song, have the children bring their name tags to the magnetic/flannel board at the end of the appropriate verse. I sang sample verses on the CD.

### What Grows in My Garden?

Oh, what grows in my garden?
Let's go out and see.
Carrots grow in my garden.
If you have one, bring it to me.

*(Repeat with tomatoes and lettuce.)*

### Tips

• Variation

  • This song can also be used as a "between book" activity by giving the children one of each vegetable.
  • Change the last line to "Show it to me." and the children can hold up the appropriate vegetable.
  • To use it as a "between book" activity, photocopy the vegetable pieces and color them. Use the carrot from "Aiken Drum" on page 139.

### Picture Book Pairings

Appelt, Kathi. *Watermelon Day.* Illustrated by Dale Gottlieb. Holt, 1996. Young Jesse waits all summer for her watermelon to ripen. (Summer)

Ehlert, Lois. *Growing Vegetable Soup*. Illustrated by author. Harcourt, 1987. A father and child grow vegetables and then make them into a soup. (Food, Gardens)

Stevens, Janet. *Tops and Bottoms*. Illustrated by author. Harcourt, 1995. Hare turns his bad luck around by striking a clever deal with the rich and lazy bear down the road. (Food, Gardens)

**Patterns Needed**

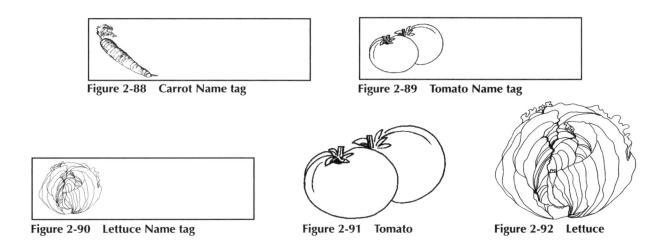

Figure 2-88   Carrot Name tag          Figure 2-89   Tomato Name tag

Figure 2-90   Lettuce Name tag         Figure 2-91   Tomato          Figure 2-92   Lettuce

**Visual Aid Creation**

1. See patterns above and on page 139 / CD files 2-88 through 2-92 and 4-13. Download and print .pdf files or photocopy them.
2. Color the vegetables.
3. Put magnets on the back.
4. Write the children's names in the blank space beside the vegetables.

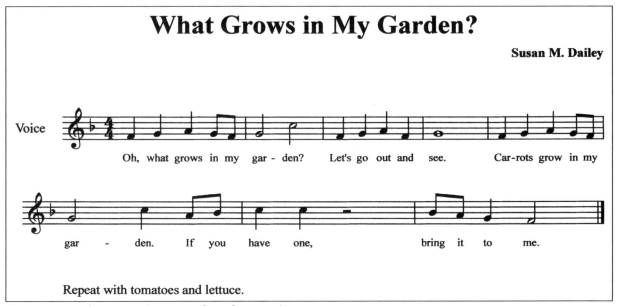

**What Grows in My Garden?**

Susan M. Dailey

Voice

Oh, what grows in my gar - den?   Let's go out and   see.   Car-rots grow in my

gar - den.   If you   have   one,   bring it to   me.

Repeat with tomatoes and lettuce.

Figure 2-93   What Grows in My Garden? sheet music

## 31. Xs AND Os

**Words and music by Susan M. Dailey**                    **Valentine's Day**

CD Track 31
Sheet Music, see page 83

### Song Presentation

You might want to sing along with the CD for this song.
Have the children move as indicated.

### Xs and Os

An X on a card
  (*Make X in air.*)
means a kiss.
  (*Blow a kiss.*)
To show a hug,
  (*Hug self.*)
make an O like this.
  (*Make O in air.*)

Xs and Os
  (*Make X and O in air.*)
on a valentine
  (*Make fingers into heart shape.*)
mean "I love you!
  (*Put hands over heart.*)
Please be mine!"

### Picture Book Pairings

Modesitt, Jeanne. *One, Two, Three, Valentine's Day.* Illustrated by Robin Spowart. Boyds Mills Press, 2002. Mister Mouse delivers Valentine gifts to his friends in this counting picture book that includes a Valentine activity.

Thompson, Lauren. *Mouse's First Valentine*. Illustrated by Buket Erdogan. Simon & Schuster, 2002. Mouse watches his sister making a valentine and wonders what it is.

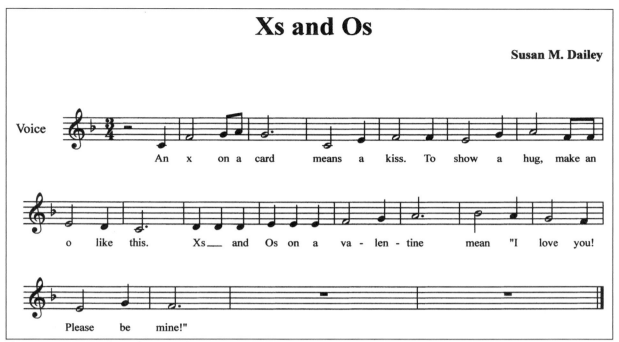

**Figure 2-94  Xs and Os sheet music**

## 32. ZOO ANIMALS

**Words and music by Susan M. Dailey**                    **Zoo, Animals**

CD Track 32

Sheet Music, see page 85

### Song Presentation

This is a Name Tag Activity.

Make a name tag for each child using the patterns on page 84.

Learn the song by listening to the CD or by playing the sheet music.

As you sing the song, have the children bring their name tags to the magnetic/flannel board at the end of the appropriate verse. I sang sample verses on the CD.

### Zoo Animals

Clap your hands! Shout hurray!
We are going to the zoo today, zoo today.

Clap your hands! Shout hurray!
I hope that we will see giraffes today.

Clap your hands! Shout hurray!
I hope that we'll see elephants today.

Clap your hands! Shout hurray!
I hope that we will see lions today.

Clap your hands! Shout hurray!
We are going to the zoo today.

## Tips

- Variation

  - This song can be used as a "between books" activity by giving the children one of each animal.
  - The children hold up the appropriate animal for each verse.

## Picture Book Pairings

Paxton, Tom. *Going to the Zoo.* Illustrated by Karen Lee Schmidt. Morrow, 1996. Enthusiastic siblings describe the animals at the "zoo, zoo, zoo." (Zoo)

Sierra, Judy. *Wild about Books*. Illustrated by Marc Brown. Knopf, 2004. The animals discover the joy of reading when a librarian mistakenly drives the book mobile to the zoo. (Animals)

## Patterns needed

**Figure 2-95   Elephant #2**

**Figure 2-96   Giraffe**

**Figure 2-97   Lion**

## Visual Aid Creation

1. See patterns above / CD files 2-95 through 2-97. Download and print .pdf files or photocopy them.
2. Copy the patterns on construction paper.
3. Put magnets on the back.

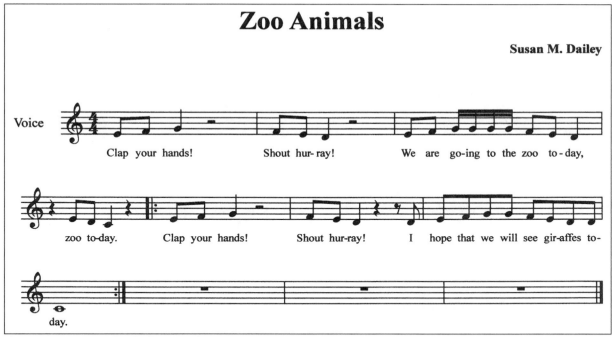

**Figure 2-98   Zoo Animals sheet music**

# CHAPTER 3

# A FRESH TAKE ON FAVORITES—NEW LYRICS TO TRADITIONAL TUNES

**1. BEFORE I GO TO BED**

**Words by Susan M. Dailey, Traditional Tune**                    **Bedtime**

CD Track 33

**Song Presentation**

Sing these words to the tune of "The Wheels on the Bus."
Have the children move as indicated.

**Before I Go to Bed**

Before I go to bed,
I take a bath.
Splash, splash, splash.
  (*Make splashing motion.*)
Splash, splash, splash.
Before I go to bed,
I take a bath.
Splash, splash, splash.

(*Continue with:*)

I brush my teeth . . . (*Make scrubbing sound.*)
I get a drink . . . Glug, glug, glug.
I read a book . . . Once upon a time . . . .
I sing a song . . . La, la, la . . . .
I give a kiss . . . (*Make kissing sound.*) . . . .
I whisper goodnight . . . Nighty-night, night . . . .

## Tips

- If you don't know this tune, "The Wheels on the Bus" can be found on *Ultimate Kids Song Collection: 101 Favorite Sing-A-Longs* by the Wonder Kids Choir.

## Picture Book Pairings

Cook, Sally. *Good Night Pillow Fight.* Illustrated by Laura Cornell. HarperCollins, 2004. A city full of parents tries to get their children to go to sleep, while the children insist on playing games.

Fox, Mem. *Time for Bed.* Illustrated by Jane Dyer. Harcourt, 1993. As darkness falls parents everywhere try to get their children ready for sleep.

## 2. BUILDING A NEW HOUSE

**Words by Susan M. Dailey, Traditional Tune**                    **Construction, Houses**

CD Track 34

## Song Presentation

Sing these words to the tune of "The Bear Went over the Mountain."

Have the children move as indicated.

### Building a New House

We are building a new house.
We are building a new house.
We are building a new house.
What will we do?
 (*Hold out hands in questioning manner.*)

What will we do?
What will we do?
We are building a new house.
What will we do?

We will dig a basement.
 (*Pretend to dig.*)
We will dig a basement.
We will dig a basement.
That's what we'll do!

We'll dig and we'll dig.
We'll dig and we'll dig.
We will dig a basement.
That's what we'll do!

*(Continue with:)*

We will saw some wood.
  *(Pretend to saw.)*

We will hammer some nails.
  *(Pretend to hammer.)*

We will tighten some screws.
  *(Make twisting motion with hand.)*

We will paint the walls.
  *(Pretend to paint.)*

### Tips

- If you don't know this tune, "The Bear Went over the Mountain" can be found on *Sing along with Bob. #1* by Bob McGrath.

### Picture Book Pairings

McDonald, Megan. *Is this a House for Hermit Crab?* Illustrated by S.D. Schindler. Orchard, 1990. When Hermit Crab outgrows his old house, he ventures out to find a new one. (Houses)

Shulman, Lisa. *Old MacDonald Had a Woodshop.* Illustrated by Ashley Wolff. Putnam, 2002. A female Old MacDonald builds a farm in her workshop. (Construction)

Suen, Anastasia. *Raise the Roof.* Illustrated by Elwood H. Smith. Viking, 2003. A family helps build their new house. (Construction, Houses)

## 3. CAPS

**Words by Susan M. Dailey, Traditional Tune**                                **Hats (Clothes), Colors**

### Song Presentation

Sing these words to the tune of "London Bridge."

This is a Name Tag Activity.

Make name tags for each child using the pattern on page 90.

As you sing the song, have the children bring their name tags to the magnetic/flannel board at the end of the appropriate verse.

After each color cap, count the number on the board. Sing the next verse filling in the correct number. I sang sample verses on the CD.

## Caps

If you have a yellow cap, yellow cap, yellow cap,
If you have a yellow cap, bring it here.

Now we have _____ yellow caps, yellow caps, yellow caps,
Now we have _____ yellow caps so let's cheer!

(*Continue with purple and orange.*)

## Tips

- If you don't know this tune, "London Bridge" can be found on *Ultimate Kids Song Collection: 101 Favorite Sing-A-Longs* by the Wonder Kids Choir.

## Picture Book Pairings

Edwards, Pamela Duncan. **Warthogs Paint.** Illustrated by Henry Cole. Hyperion, 2001. As some warthogs spend a rainy day painting their kitchen, they make a mess and learn about mixing colors. (Colors)

Fox, Mem. **The Magic Hat.** Illustrated by Tricia Tusa. Harcourt, 2002. A wizard's hat blows into town, changing people into different animals when it lands on their heads. (Hats)

Taback, Simms. **Joseph Had a Little Overcoat.** Illustrated by author. Viking, 1999. A very old overcoat is recycled numerous times into a variety of garments. (Clothes)

## Patterns Needed

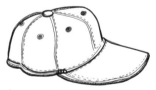

**Figure 3-1    Cap**

## Visual Aid Creation

1. See pattern above / CD file 3-1. Download and print the .pdf file or photocopy it.
2. Copy the pattern on yellow, purple and orange paper.
3. Put magnets on the back.

## 4. CAR SOUNDS

**Words by Susan M. Dailey, Traditional Tune**                    **Cars (Vehicles), Sounds**

CD Track 35

### Song Presentation

Sing these words to the tune of "Shoo, Fly."

Have the children move and make the sounds as indicated.

### Car Sounds

My car makes lots of sounds.
  (*On "car," pretend to drive, on "noises" put hand to ear.*)
My car makes lots of sounds.
My car makes lots of sounds.
Listen while it makes these sounds.

My seat belt goes click . . .
  (*Pretend to fasten seat belt.*)
Listen while it goes click.

My horn goes beep, beep, beep . . .
  (*On "beep, beep," pretend to honk horn.*)
Listen while it goes beep, beep.

My turn light goes (*Make clicking noise with tongue.*) . . .
  (*On clicking noise, open fingers rhythmically.*)
Listen while it goes (make clicking noise with tongue).

My engine goes vroom, vroom . . .
  (*Pretend to drive.*)
Listen while it goes vroom.

### Tips

- If you don't know this tune, "Shoo, Fly" can be found on *Ultimate Kids Song Collection: 101 Favorite Sing-A-Longs* by the Wonder Kids Choir.
- When you sing the verse about the turn light, you can change the sound of the clicks by changing the shape of your mouth. I pucker my lips on the first click and then pull them outward in a smile.

### Picture Book Pairings

Macdonald, Ross. *Achoo! Bang! Crash!: A Noisy Alphabet.* Illustrated by author. Roaring Brook, 2003. Words about sound and noise illustrate the letters of the alphabet. (Sounds)

Zane, Alex. *The Wheels on the Race Car.* Illustrated by James Warhola. Orchard, 2005. Animal race car drivers roar around the track. (Cars)

## 5. CARS

**Words by Susan M. Dailey, Traditional Tune**           **Cars (Vehicles), Colors**

### Song Presentation

Sing these words to the tune of "Hush Little Baby."

This is a Name Tag Activity.

Make name tags for each child using the pattern below /CD file 3-2.

As you sing the song, have the children bring their name tags to the magnetic/flannel board at the end of the appropriate verse.

Count the number on the board. Sing the song again, filling in the correct number.

### Cars

Beep, beep! Honk, honk goes the car,
but we have just one so far.
So, please bring the red ones here
and we'll give a great big cheer.

(*Repeat with other colors.*)

### Tips

- If you don't know this tune, "Hush Little Baby" can be found on *Ultimate Kids Song Collection: 101 Favorite Sing-A-Longs* by the Wonder Kids Choir.
- The number of different colors of cars will determine how many times you have to sing the song. I recommend three to five colors.

### Picture Book Pairings

Barton, Byron. *My Car.* Illustrated by author. Greenwillow, 2001. Sam describes in loving detail his car and how he drives it. (Cars)

Crews, Donald. *Freight Train.* Illustrated by author. Mulberry Books, 1992. Brief text and illustrations trace the journey of a colorful train as it goes through tunnels, by cities, and over trestles. (Colors)

### Patterns Needed

Figure 3-2   **Car**

### Visual Aid Creation

1. See pattern above / CD file 3-2. Download and print the .pdf file or photocopy it.
2. Copy the pattern on various colors.
3. Put magnets on the back.

## 6. CLOWNS GALORE

**Words by Susan M. Dailey, Traditional Tune**                                    **Circus**

### Song Presentation

Sing these words to the tune of "This Old Man."

This is a Name Tag Activity.

Make name tags for each child using the patterns on page xx.

As you sing the song, have a few of the children bring their name tags to the magnetic/flannel board.

Count the number on the board. Sing the song again, filling in the correct number.

### Clowns Galore

Clowns galore, clowns galore,
riding in a circus car.
Here's one clown,
but now I need some more.
Bring your clown up to the board.

Clowns galore, clowns galore,
riding in a circus car.
Here's _____ clowns,
But now I need some more.
Bring your clown up to the board.

### Tips

- If you don't know this tune, "This Old Man" can be found on *Ultimate Kids Song Collection: 101 Favorite Sing-A-Longs* by the Wonder Kids Choir.

### Picture Book Pairings

Downs, Mike. *You See a Circus, I See . . .* Illustrated by McGrory, Anik. Charlesbridge, 2005. A young boy, who is a member of an acrobat family, describes the people and activities of his circus home.

Paul, Ann Whitford. *Little Monkey Says Good Night.* Illustrated by David Walker. Farrar, 2003. When Little Monkey says good night to the performers in the big top tent, he creates a circus act of his own.

Figure 3-3  Clown Sample

**Figure 3-4   Clown Patterns**

**Patterns Needed**

**Visual Aid Creation**

1. See patterns / CD file 3-4. Download and print .pdf files or photocopy them.
2. Trace the pattern pieces on construction paper. Assemble pieces.
3. Put magnets on the back.

## 7. COUNTING SHEEP

**Words by Susan M. Dailey, Traditional Tune**          **Bedtime, Sheep (Animals), Parents (Families)**

CD Track 36

### Song Presentation

Sing these words to the tune of "This Old Man."

### Counting Sheep

Counting sheep,
  (*Point and pretend to count.*)
counting sheep
helps my mommy
go to sleep.
  (*Stretch and yawn.*)

One sheep, two sheep,
  (*Hold up appropriate number of fingers.*)
three sheep, four—
Soon my mommy
starts to snore.
  (*Snore.*)

(*Repeat, replacing "mommy" with "daddy."*)

## Tips

- If you don't know this tune, "This Old Man" can be found on *Ultimate Kids Song Collection: 101 Favorite Sing-A-Longs* by the Wonder Kids Choir.
- When we sing about Daddy, we snore very loudly. In fairness to fathers, I explain that not all Dads snore loudly.
- You might want to explain the idea behind counting sheep, since this is a concept with which young children might not be familiar.
- Variation

    - You could also add verses about brothers, sisters, dogs, etc.

## Picture Book Pairings

Fox, Mem and Judy Horacek. *Where is the Green Sheep?* Illustrated by Judy Horacek. Harcourt, 2004. A story about many different sheep, and one that seems to be missing. (Sheep)

Markes, Julie. *Shhhhh! Everybody's Sleeping.* Illustrated by David Parkins. HarperCollins, 2005. A young child is encouraged to go to sleep by the thought of everyone else sleeping, from teacher to baker to postman. (Bedtime)

Scotton, Rob. *Russell the Sheep.* Illustrated by author. HarperCollins, 2005. Russell the sheep tries all different ways to get to sleep. (Sheep)

## 8. CRAYON BOX

**Words by Susan M. Dailey, Traditional Tune**                **Colors, Art, Toys/Playing**

CD Track 37

### Song Presentation

Sing these words to the tune of "Ten Little Indians."

Put together the visual aid, using the pattern on page 96.

Put the crayons on the board as you sing the first verse.

Point to the appropriate colored crayon as you sing the second verse.

### Crayon Box

One big crayon, two big crayons,
Three big crayons, four big crayons,
Five big crayons, six big crayons,
Seven and eight big crayons.

Red one, yellow one, blue one, green one,
Orange one, purple one, black and brown ones—
many colors of the rainbow
in my crayon box.

### Tips

- If you don't know this tune, the sheet music for "Ten Little Indians" can be found in *The Big Book of Children's Songs* published by the Hal Leonard Corporation. "Peter, James and John in a Sailboat" is sung to the same tune, which can be found on *More Sunday Morning Songs with Bob & Larry: VeggieTales Sing-alongs.*

### Picture Book Pairings

Beaumont, Karen. *I Ain't Gonna Paint No More!* Illustrated by David Catrow. Harcourt, 2005. In the rhythm of a familiar folk song, a child cannot resist adding one more dab of paint in surprising places. (Art)

Hoena, B. A. *Toys ABC.* Illustrated by author. Capstone, 2005. Introduces toys through photographs and brief text that uses one word relating to toys for each letter of the alphabet. (Toys/Playing)

Seeger, Laura Vaccaro. *Lemons are Not Red.* Illustrated by author. Roaring Brook, 2004. A simple story highlights such things as a yellow lemon, a pink flamingo, and a silver moon in a visual game in which die-cut shapes fall on the correct color backgrounds. (Colors)

### Patterns Needed

**Figure 3-5   Crayon**

### Visual Aid Creation

1. See page pattern above / CD file 3-5. Download and print the .pdf file or photocopy it.
2. Copy the pattern on the various colors mentioned in the song.
3. Put magnets on the back.

### 9. CRAYONS

**Words by Susan M. Dailey, Traditional Tune**                **Colors, Art, Toys/Playing**

CD Track 38

### Song Presentation

Sing these words to the tune of "If You're Happy and You Know It."

Make up crayons for each child in the seven colors mentions using the patterns on page 97.

Have the children act out the motions with the crayons as indicated.

### Crayons

If you have a crayon red, crayon red,
If you have a crayon red, crayon red,
If you have a crayon red,
please put it on your head.
If you have a crayon red, crayon red.

If you have a crayon blue . . .
. . . please put it on your shoe . . .

If you have a crayon green . . .
. . . wave it high so it is seen . . .

If you have a crayon yellow . . .
. . . make it wiggle just like Jell-o® . . .

If you have a crayon black . . .
. . . hide it behind your back . . .

If you have a crayon brown . . .
. . . fly it up and fly it down . . .

If you have a crayon white . . .
. . . shake it left and shake it right . . .

### Tips

- If you don't know this tune, "If You're Happy and You Know It" can be found on *Sing along with Bob. #1* by Bob McGrath.
- You can color manila envelopes to look like crayon boxes and put the crayons inside.
- Variation

    - Give each child real crayons in the colors mentioned in the song.

### Picture Book Pairings

Gilliland, Judith Heide. *Not in the House, Newton!* Illustrated by Elizabeth Sayles. Clarion, 1995. Everything Newton draws with his magic red crayon becomes real, and, heeding his mother's admonition, he flies the airplane he draws right out the window. (Art)

Hubbard, Patricia. *My Crayons Talk.* Illustrated by G. Brian Karas. Holt, 1999. Brown crayon sings "Play, Mud pie day," and Blue crayon calls "Sky, Swing so high" in this story about talking crayons. (Colors)

Willems, Mo. *Knuffle Bunny.* Illustrated by author. Hyperion, 2004. After Trixie and daddy leave the laundromat, something very important turns up missing. (Toys/Playing)

### Patterns Needed

- Crayon pattern

### Visual Aid Creation

1. Use the crayon on page 96 / CD file 3-5 for the pattern. Download and print the .pdf file or photocopy it.
2. Copy the pattern on various colors.

## 10. DO YOU HAVE A LADYBUG?

**Words by Susan M. Dailey, Traditional Tune**                                    **Bugs, Summer**

CD Track 39

### Song Presentation

Sing these words to the tune of "Muffin Man."

Make the four bugs for each child using the patterns on page 99.

Pass out the bug pieces before singing the song.

Have the children act out the words with the bugs as indicated.

### Do You Have a Ladybug?

Do you have a ladybug,
a ladybug, a ladybug?
If you have a ladybug,
put it on your head.

Do you have a bumblebee,
a bumblebee, a bumblebee?
If you have a bumblebee,
buzz it all around.

Do you have a cricket,
a cricket, a cricket?
If you have a cricket,
put it on your toe.

Do you have a butterfly,
a butterfly, a butterfly?
If you have a butterfly,
toss it in the air.

### Tips

• If you don't know this tune, "Muffin Man" can be found on *Songs Children Love to Sing* by Ella Jenkins.

- I didn't always sing the verses in the same order and we sometimes did different things with the bugs.
- We finished the activity by singing, "If you have a ladybug, put it in the jar" and continued with the other three bugs.
- Variation

    - You can give each child just one or two of the bugs.
    - I gave everyone a plastic peanut butter jar with all the bugs inside. The kids removed the bugs from the jar at the beginning of the song and used the appropriate one for each verse.

### Picture Book Pairings

Barner, Bob. ***Bugs! Bugs! Bugs!*** Illustrated by author. Chronicle, 1999. A nonsense rhyme introduces children to familiar insects. (Bugs)

London, Jonathan. ***Sun Dance, Water Dance.*** Illustrated by Greg Couch. Dutton, 2001. Celebrates a great summer day of childhood near and in a river. (Summer)

### Patterns Needed

**Figure 3-6    Bumblebee**

**Figure 3-7    Butterfly #1**

**Figure 3-8    Ladybug**

**Figure 3-9    Cricket**

### Visual Aid Creation

1. See patterns above / CD files 3-6 through 3-9. Download and print .pdf files or photocopy them.
2. Color the pieces.

## 11. DO YOU KNOW WHAT TIME IT IS?

**Words by Susan M. Dailey, Traditional Tune**

CD Track 40

### Song Presentation

Sing these words to the tune of "Muffin Man."
This is a Closing Song.

**Do You Know What Time It Is?**

Do you know what time it is,
  (*Tap pretend watch.*)
time it is, time it is?
Do you know what time it is?
Storytime is over.

Now's the time to wave goodbye,
  (*Wave hand.*)
wave goodbye, wave goodbye.
Now's the time to wave goodbye,
Storytime is over.

Now's the time to stand up tall,
  (*Stand up.*)
Stand up tall, stand up tall.
Now's the time to stand up tall.
Storytime is over.

But come back and see us soon,
see us soon, see us soon.
But come back and see us soon,
when the fun will start again.

### Tips

- If you don't know this tune, "Muffin Man" can be found on *Songs Children Love to Sing* by Ella Jenkins.
- On the last line, I slow down.
- On the word "again" I begin with a very low note and slide up the scale. As simple as this sounds, the children love it and it's become my signature song.

## 12. EARTH SONG

**Words by Amy Greiner, Traditional Tune**                                             **Summer**

### Song Presentation

Sing these words to the tune of "Frère Jacques."

This is a Name Tag Activity.

Make name tags for each child using the patterns on page 102.

As you sing the song, have the children bring their name tags to the magnetic/flannel board at the end of the appropriate verse.

### Earth Song

Yellow sunshine, yellow sunshine,
warm and bright, warm and bright.
Put them on the board now, put them on the board now,
on the left, on the right.

Fluffy clouds, fluffy clouds
Floating by, floating by—
put them on the board now, put them on the board now,
some down low, some up high.

Leaves of green, leaves of green
on the trees, on the trees:
put them on the board now, put them on the board now,
if you please, if you please.

Pretty flowers, pretty flowers,
watch them bloom, watch them bloom.
Put them on the board now, put them on the board now.
Is there room? Is there room?

*—written by Amy Greiner, Wells County Public Library*

### Tips

- If you don't know this tune, "Frère Jacques" can be found on *Ultimate Kids Song Collection: 101 Favorite Sing-A-Longs* by the Wonder Kids Choir.

### Picture Book Pairings

Gray, Rita. ***Nonna's Porch.*** Illustrated by Terry Widener. Hyperion, 2004. Nonna experiences all the sounds of summer from her porch.

### Patterns Needed

**Figure 3-10   Sun #1**

**Figure 3-11   Cloud**

**Figure 3-12   Leaf #1**

**Figure 3-13   Flower #1**

### Visual Aid Creation

1. See patterns above / CD files 3-10 through 3-13. Download and print .pdf files or photocopy them.
2. Copy the pattern on appropriate colors.
3. Put magnets on the back.

## 13. FISH TANK

**Words by Susan M. Dailey, Traditional Tune**                                    **Fish, Pets**

CD Track 41

### Song Presentation

Sing these words to the tune of "Jack and Jill."

Construct the visual aid using the fish pattern on page 104 and the cat from "Kitty Cat, Pounce" on page 37.

Pause and let the children fill in the number that finishes the rhymes.

When you get to the last line, bring out the cat puppet. When it gets near the fish bowl, say, "Scat, cat!" Hide it behind your back.

Bring it out again several times and encourage the kids to help scare off the cat, a task they love.

**Fish Tank**

On Saturday, I got my wish
when I found a tank for a fish.

But an empty tank is not much fun,
so I bought a fish, and now I have one.

I have one fish, but that won't do,
so I bought another, and now I have two.

I have two fish swimming happily,
but I bought another, and now I have three.

I have three fish, but I want more.
So I bought another, and now I have four.

I have four fish that jump and dive.
But I bought another and now I have five.

On Saturday, I got my wish
when I found a tank for a fish.

A tank full of fish is lots of fun.
But the cat just saw them—so I'd better run!

Scat, cat! (*spoken*)

## Tips

- If you don't know this tune, "Jack and Jill" can be found on *Ultimate Kids Song Collection: 101 Favorite Sing-A-Longs* by the Wonder Kids Choir.
- Variation

  - Instead of using a box to create the visual aid, you could also get a picture frame or picture frame mat.
  - Cutting a frame from poster board would also work. Make the frame wide enough to "hide" the fish until they are needed.

## Picture Book Pairings

Bennett, Kelly. *Not Norman: A Goldfish Story.* Illustrated by Noah Z. Jones. Candlewick, 2005. As a boy attempts to convince someone else to take his disappointing pet, he learns to love Norman the goldfish himself. (Fish, Pets)
Sayre, April Pulley. *Trout, Trout, Trout!: A Fish Chant.*

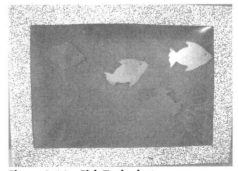

**Figure 3-14  Fish Tank photo**

Illustrated by Trip Park. NorthWord Press, 2004. Presents a rhyme and information about a variety of freshwater fish found in North America north of Mexico. (Fish)

## Patterns Needed

- Fish
- Cat

**Figure 3-15    Fish #1**

### Visual Aid Creation

1. See pattern / CD file 3-15. Download and print the .pdf file or photocopy it.
2. Trace the pattern to make 5 fish. Copy the cat pattern.
3. Attach the cat to a tongue depressor.
4. To make the fish tank, I found a lid to a gray stationery box. A shoe box lid would also work.
5. Cut out the center, leaving only a small edge all the way around.
6. Cover the opening with clear plastic. I used left over laminator film.
7. Suspend the fish from the top of the box using fishing line.
8. Lay the fish on the top of the prop before you "put them in the tank." You can use a small amount of poster putty to keep them from falling off the side.

## 14. HOORAY FOR WINTER!

**Words by Susan M. Dailey, Traditional Tune**                                    **Winter**

CD Track 42

### Song Presentation

Sing these words to the tune of "London Bridge."

Have the children act out the words as indicated.

### Hooray for Winter!

Snow is falling all around,
  (*Fluttering fingers downward.*)
All around, all around.
Snow is falling all around.
Hooray for winter!

Now put on your boots and hat.
  (*Touch toes, then head.*)
Boots and hat, boots and hat.
Now put on your boots and hat.
Hooray for winter!

Take the snow and roll it round,
  (*Roll hands around each other.*)
Roll it round, roll it round.
Take the snow and roll it round,
Hooray for winter!

Now, let's have a snowball fight,
  (*Pretend to throw.*)
Snowball fight, snowball fight.
Now, let's have a snowball fight,
Hooray for winter!

## Tips

- If you don't know this tune, "London Bridge" can be found on *Ultimate Kids Song Collection: 101 Favorite Sing-A-Longs* by the Wonder Kids Choir.
- You can ask the children what else they do in winter and make up additional verses using their suggestions.

## Picture Book Pairings

Wilson, Karma. *Bear Snores On.* Illustrated by Jane Chapman. Gardners Books, 2001. On a cold winter night many animals gather to party in the cave of a sleeping bear, who then awakes and protests that he has missed the food and the fun.

## 15. I AM A PIRATE, IT'S TRUE

**Words by Susan M. Dailey, Traditional Tune**                    **Pirates**

CD Track 43

### Song Presentation

Sing these words to the tune of "The Bear Went over the Mountain."
Have the children move as indicated.

### I Am a Pirate, It's True

I am a pirate, it's true.
  (*Point to self, then nod head.*)
I've sailed the ocean blue.
  (*Move hand in waving motion.*)
With a parrot on my shoulder,
  (*Point to shoulder.*)
No one could be bolder.
  (*Hook thumbs through shirt.*)

No one could be bolder!
No one could be bolder!
With a parrot on my shoulder,
no one could be bolder.

I am a pirate, it's true.
I've sailed the ocean blue.
With a patch over my eye,
  (*Place hand over eye.*)
No one's as mean as I.
  (*Scowl.*)

No one's as mean as I.
No one's as mean as I.
With a patch over my eye,
no one's as mean as I.

I am a pirate, it's true.
I've sailed the ocean blue.
So if you see me coming,
  (*Place hand over eyes, look around.*)
You'd better start a-running.
  (*Slap hands against legs.*)

You'd better start a-running.
You'd better start a-running.
So if you see me coming,
you'd better start a-running.


## Tips

- If you don't know this tune, "The Bear Went over the Mountain" can be found on *Sing along with Bob. #1* by Bob McGrath.
- Pause at the end of the second to last line. Then sing the last line very quickly.


## Picture Book Pairings

Sturges, Philemon. ***This Little Pirate.*** Illustrated by Amy Walrod. Dutton, 2005. Two bands of pirates fight over a box, but when they raise the white flag and open the box together, they find a treasure to share.

## 16. I LIKE

**Words by Susan M. Dailey, Traditional Tune**                     **Valentine's Day, Love**

CD Track 44

### Song Presentation

Sing these words to the tune of "Yankee Doodle."

Use the patterns to create graphics.

Put the graphics on the board to help the children remember the words.

Have the children move as indicated.

### I Like

I like the sun
  (*Make circle with arms above head.*)
and I like rain.
  (*Wiggle fingers and move downward.*)
I like planes
  (*Move hand upward.*)
and I like trains.
  (*Move arms in circular motion by sides.*)

I like ice cream
  (*Pretend to lick ice cream cone.*)
and bubble gum, too.
  (*Pretend to chew gum.*)
I like those things,
  (*Nod head.*)
But I love you!
  (*Put hands over heart.*)

### Tips

- If you don't know this tune, "Yankee Doodle" can be found on *Ultimate Kids Song Collection: 101 Favorite Sing-A-Longs* by the Wonder Kids Choir.
- Variation

  - This can be done just with hands motions.

### Picture Book Pairings

***Rodgers and Hammerstein's My Favorite Things.*** Illustrated by Rene Graef. HarperCollins, 2000. An illustrated version of the popular song enumerating favorite things, from raindrops on roses to silver-white winters melting into springs. (Love)

Rylant, Cynthia. ***If You'll Be My Valentine.*** Illustrated by Fumi Kosaka. HarperCollins, 2004. A little boy gives out Valentines to friends and family. (Valentine's Day)

## Patterns Needed

**Figure 3-16    Sun #2**

**Figure 3-17    Rain #1**

**Figure 3-18    Airplane**

**Figure 3-19    Train**

**Figure 3-20    Bubble Gum**

### Visual Aid Creation

1. See patterns above / CD files 3-16 through 3-20. Download and print .pdf files or photo-copy them.
2. Copy the pattern.
3. Put magnets on the back.

## 17. I'M A SCHOOL BUS

**Words by Susan M. Dailey, Traditional Tune**                    **Buses (Vehicles), School**

CD Track 45

### Song Presentation

Sing these words to the tune of "Clementine."

Have the children move as indicated.

### I'm a School Bus

I am long.
(*Stretch arms in front of body.*)

And I am tall.
   (*Stretch arms high.*)
And I am very, very wide.
   (*Stretch arms out to sides.*)
I am yellow
With black numbers
And a stop arm on my side.
   (*Palm facing out, then move it to side.*)

I'm a school bus.
   (*Point to self, nod head.*)
I'm a school bus.
Yes, I am a school bus.
I'm a school bus.
I'm a school bus.
I'm a very, cool school bus.
   (*Put two thumbs up.*)

### Tips

- If you don't know this tune, "Clementine" can be found on *Ultimate Kids Song Collection: 101 Favorite Sing-A-Longs* by the Wonder Kids Choir.

### Picture Book Pairings

Roth, Carol. *Little School Bus.* Illustrated by Pamela Paparone. North-South, 2002. An assortment of animals, including a goat in a coat, a quick chick, and a hairy bear, ride the bus to and from school.

Willems, Mo. *Don't Let the Pigeon Drive the Bus.* Illustrated by author. Hyperion, 2003. A pigeon dreams of driving a bus and begs the audience to allow it.

## 18. IN AND OUT THE DOORS

**Words by Susan M. Dailey, Traditional Tune**                                    **Houses**

CD Track 46

### Song Presentation

Sing these words to the tune of "Go In and Out the Window."

This is a Stretch where the children have a chance to move around between stories.

Have the children stand up and move as indicated.

### In and Out the Doors

Step in and out the front door.
   (*Take a step forward, then back.*)

Step in and out the front door.
Step in and out the front door.
Then make a doorbell sound.

Jump in and out the back door.
  (*Jump backwards, then forwards.*)
Jump in and out the back door.
Jump in and out the back door.
Bend down and touch the ground.

Slide in and out the side door.
  (*Slide to one side, then to other.*)
Slide in and out the side door.
Slide in and out the side door.
And then, turn all around.

Step in and out the front door.
Jump in and out the back door.
Slide in and out the side door.
Then sit yourself right down.

## Tips

- If you don't know this tune, "Go In and Out the Window" can be found on *Wee Sing Silly Songs* by the Pamela Conn Beale and Susan Hagen Nipp.
- Before I begin the fourth verse, I usually tell the kids that they'll have to listen very closely or I'll fool them.

## Picture Book Pairings

Juster, Norton. ***The Hello, Goodbye Window***. Illustrated by Chris Raschka. Hyperion, 2005. A little girl describes the magic kitchen window in her grandparents' home.

## 19. KITES

**Words by Susan M. Dailey, Traditional Tune**                    **Kites, Wind, Spring**

CD Track 47

## Song Presentation

Sing these words to the tune of "99 Bottles of Pop."
Make the visual aid using the pattern provided on page 112.

## Kites

Four kites up in the air,
four kites in the air.
One kite flew too close to a tree.
Now the kite's stuck there.

(*Repeat with three, two and one. Then sing:*)

Four kites up in a tree,
four kites in a tree.
The wind blew hard and harder still.
The kites fell down to me.

## Picture Book Pairings

Asch, Frank and Devin Asch. ***Like a Windy Day***. Illustrated by authors. Harcourt, 2002. A young girl discovers all the things the wind can do, by playing and dancing along with it. (Wind)

Lin, Grace. ***Kite Flying***. Illustrated by author. Knopf, 2002. A girl describes how her family makes and flies a kite. (Kites)

Seuling, Barbara. ***Spring Song***. Illustrated by Greg Newbold. Harcourt, 2001. When new leaves sprout, buds appear, cocoons burst open, and other signs announce the coming of spring, various animals from bears to bullfrogs respond to the warmth of the season. (Spring)

## Patterns Needed

• Kite

## Visual Aid Creation

**Figure 3-21   Kite and Tree photo**

1. See page 112 / CD file 3-22 for the pattern. Download and print the .pdf file or photocopy it.
2. Use the pattern to make four kites from construction paper, poster board or craft foam.
3. Add a tail with yarn or ribbon.
4. Use a hot glue gun to attach powerful magnets on the back of the kites.
5. Attach spools or craft wheels to four other magnets also using a hot glue gun. The spools or wheels are to provide a handle that will allow you to move the kites around the board.
6. Make a tree on either light weight illustration board or heavy weight poster board. If you use poster board, it would be good to mount it in a poster frame to give it stability.
7. I made my tree by using a leaf stamp to place leaves of various shades of green in one corner of the board. I then added branches with brown marker.

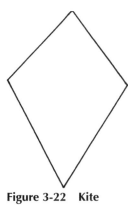

**Figure 3-22  Kite**

8. Laminate the board so that the kites move easily across it.

9. Hold the kites to the board by making contact with one of the magnets on the back side. Make sure that they make a solid connection.

10. By moving the magnet on the back carefully, the kite can be "flown" down into the tree. Sometimes I turn the magnet on the back so that the kite makes a complete circle on the board before flying it into the tree.

11. On the final line, pull the magnets away from the back of the board. The kites will fall to the floor.

## 20. LITTLE BIRDS

**Words by Susan M. Dailey, Traditional Tune**                                    **Birds, Spring**

### Song Presentation

Sing these words to the tune of "Bluebird, Bluebird."

This is a Name Tag Activity.

Make name tags for each child using the patterns on page 113.

As you sing the song, have the children bring their name tags to the magnetic/flannel board at the end of the appropriate verse.

### Little Birds

Little birds, little birds,
fly to my window.
Little birds, little birds,
fly to my window.
Little birds, little birds,
fly to my window.
Fly to my window, robins.

(*Repeat with blue jays and cardinals.*)

### Tips

• If you don't know the tune, "Bluebird, Bluebird" can be found on *Mainly Mother Goose* by Sharon, Lois and Bram.

### Picture Book Pairings

Hubbell, Patricia. ***Hurray for Spring!*** Illustrated by Taia Morley. NorthWord, 2005. A young boy cele-brates all the things he can do in the spring in this rhyming story. (Spring)

Peters, Lisa Westberg. ***Cold Little Duck, Duck, Duck.*** Illustrated by Sam Williams. Greenwillow, 2000. Early one spring a little duck arrives at her pond and finds it still frozen, but not for long. (Spring)

Winer, Yvonne. ***Birds Build Nests.*** Illustrated by Tony Oliver. Charlesbridge, 2002. Describes how, where, why, and when birds around the world build nests. (Birds)

### Patterns Needed

**Figure 3-23   Robin**

**Figure 3-24   Blue Jay**

**Figure 3-25   Cardinal**

### Visual Aid Creation

1. See patterns above / CD file 3-23 through 3-25. Download and print .pdf files or photocopy them.
2. Color the patterns.
3. Put magnets on the back.

## 21. MY BIKE

**Words by Susan M. Dailey, Traditional Tune**                    **Bicycles (Vehicles), Toys/Playing**

CD Track 48

### Song Presentation

Sing these words to the tune of "The Farmer in the Dell."

You can sing this several times, getting faster each time through.

Have the children move as indicated.

### My Bike

Pedal 'round and 'round,
  (*Roll hands around each other.*)
pedal 'round and 'round.
I steer my bike
  (*Pretend to steer.*)

anywhere I like.
Pedal 'round and 'round.

## Tips

- If you don't know this tune, "The Farmer in the Dell" can be found on *Ultimate Kids Song Collection: 101 Favorite Sing-A-Longs* by the Wonder Kids Choir.

## Picture Book Pairings

McLeod, Emilie Warren. ***The Bear's Bicycle***. Illustrated by David McPhail. Little, Brown, 1986. A boy and his bear have an exciting bicycle ride.

## 22. OH, I WORK AT THE ZOO

**Words by Susan M. Dailey, Traditional Tune**                                    **Zoo, Animals, Jobs**

CD Track 49

### Song Presentation

Sing these words to the tune of "She'll Be Coming 'Round the Mountain."

### Oh, I Work at the Zoo

Oh, I work at the zoo. Yes, I do. Yes, I do.
Oh, I work at the zoo. Yes, I do. Yes, I do.
Oh, I work at the zoo. Yes, I work at the zoo.
Oh, I work at the zoo. Yes, I do. Yes, I do.

Oh, I clean the lions' cages. Yes, I do. Sweep, sweep . . .

Oh, I feed the penguins fish. Yes, I do. Yum, yum, sweep, sweep . . .

Oh, I give the bears a bath. Yes, I do. Splish, splash, yum, yum, sweep, sweep . . .

Oh, I trim the tigers' toenails. Yes, I do. Clip, clip, splish, splash, yum, yum, sweep, sweep . . .

### Tips

- If you don't know this tune, "She'll Be Coming 'Round the Mountain" can be found on *Ultimate Kids Song Collection: 101 Favorite Sing-A-Longs* by the Wonder Kids Choir.
- Variation
  - You can add motions by pretending to do the various tasks.
  - For younger children, you might not want to add the final words from the earlier verses at the end of each line.

### Picture Book Pairings

Butler, John. *Whose Baby Am I?* Illustrated by author. Viking, 2001. Pages picturing animal babies are each followed by a page with the baby, its mother, and their names. (Animals)

Massie, Diane Redfield. *The Baby Beebee Bird*. Illustrated by Steven Kellogg. HarperCollins, 2000. The zoo animals find a way to keep the baby beebee bird awake during the day so that they can get some sleep at night. (Zoo)

Miller, Margaret. *Guess Who?* Illustrated by author. Greenwillow, 1994. A child is asked who delivers the mail, gives haircuts, flies an airplane, and performs other important tasks. Each question has several different answers from which to choose. (Jobs)

## 23. OH, LET'S SING A SONG OF STORYTIME

**Words by Susan M. Dailey, Traditional Tune**                         **Names**

CD Track 50

### Song Presentation

Sing these words to the tune of "The More We Get Together."

This is a Welcome Activity.

Insert the children's names into the blanks. I sang some sample names on the CD.

### Oh, Let's Sing a Song of Storytime

Oh, let's sing a song of storytime,
of storytime, of storytime.
Oh, let's sing a song of storytime.
I'm glad that you're here.

Hello, ———, hello, ———.
Hello, ———, hello, ———.
Oh, let's sing a song of storytime.
I'm glad that you're here.

### Tips

- If you don't know this tune, "The More We Get Together" can be found on *Sing along with Bob. #1* by Bob McGrath.
- If the number of children isn't divisible by four, you could also sing hello to everybody, to the grownups, or to yourself.
- You might want to shake the children's hands as you sing their names.

### Picture Book Pairings

Catalanotto, Peter. *Matthew A. B. C.* Illustrated by author. Atheneum, 2002. A new boy named Matthew joins Mrs. Tuttle's class, which already has twenty-five students whose first names are Matthew and whose last names begin with every letter except Z.

## 24. ONE LITTLE PENGUIN

**Words by Susan M. Dailey, Traditional Tune**                    **Penguins (Birds), Winter**

### Song Presentation

Sing these words to the tune of "Five Little Ducks."

This is a Name Tag Activity.

Make a name tag for each child, using the patterns on page 119.

Have the children stand up and act out the words as indicated.

As you sing the song, have a few of the children bring their name tags to the magnetic/flannel board.

Count the number on the board. Sing the song again, filling in the correct number.

### One Little Penguin

One little penguin in the snow
waddles fast and waddles slow,
  (*Waddle.*)
flaps his wings and calls, "Come on,
  (*Flap arms, put hand beside mouth as if calling.*)
Join me in this winter fun!"
  (*Beckon with hand.*)
———— little penguins in the snow
waddle fast and waddle slow,
flap their wings and call, "Come on,
join us in this winter fun!"

### Tips

• If you don't know this tune, "Five Little Ducks" can be found on *Raffi's Box of Sunshine* by Raffi.

### Picture Book Pairings

Dunrea, Olivier. *It's Snowing.* Illustrated by author. Farrar, 2002. A mother shares the magic of a snowy night with her baby. (Winter)

Lester, Helen. *Tacky the Penguin.* Illustrated by Lynn Munsinger. Houghton Mifflin, 1988. Tacky the penguin does not fit in with his sleek and graceful companions, but his odd behavior comes in handy when hunters come with maps and traps. (Penguins)

### Patterns Needed

- Penguin patterns

### Visual Aid Creation

1. Use the patterns from "Penguin Baby" on page 119 / CD files 3-27 through 3-30 for the patterns. Download and print .pdf files or photocopy them.
2. Trace the patterns and assemble the pieces.
3. Put magnets on the back.

## 25. PENGUIN BABY

**Words by Susan M. Dailey, Traditional Tune**                    **Penguins (Birds), Winter**

CD Track 51

### Song Presentation

Sing these words to the tune of "The More We Get Together."

Make the visual aid, using the patterns provided on page 119.

You need to make three large penguins and one small.

You need a tray, table or other flat surface for this activity.

Place the small penguin under one of the large ones, without the children seeing it, before you start singing.

Sing the first verse.

Pick up the penguins one at a time as you sing the second verse, waiting to show the baby to the audience on the second line.

During the third verse, move the penguins around.

On the last line, ask the children which penguin has the baby under it. This activity is like the shell game; however, I want the children to be able to identify the correct penguin, so I move them slowly.

### Penguin Baby

One penguin has a baby,
a baby, a baby.
One penguin has a baby
sitting on its feet.
Is it this one? Is it this one?
No, it is this one.

This penguin has a baby
sitting on its feet.

Now the penguins waddle.
They waddle. They waddle.
Now the penguins waddle.
Where is the baby?

## Tips

- If you don't know this tune, "The More We Get Together" can be found on *Sing along with Bob. #1* by Bob McGrath. You could even do the activity without singing the song.
- Variation

  - You can do the activity without using the song.
  - I was able to find a small toy penguin to use for the baby instead of making one.

## Picture Book Pairings

Jenkins, Martin. *The Emperor's Egg.* Illustrated by Jane Chapman. Candlewick, 1999. Describes the parental behavior of Emperor penguins, emphasizing how the male keeps the egg warm until it hatches and how the parents care for the chick after it is born. (Penguins)

Vestergaard, Hope. *Hello, Snow!* Illustrated by Nadine Bernard Westcott. Farrar, 2004. A young child bundles up and discovers the delights of a snowy day. (Winter)

**Figure 3-26    Penguin photo**

## Patterns Needed

- Penguin patterns

## Visual Aid Creation

1. See page 119 / CD files 3-27 through 3-30 for the pattern. Download and print .pdf files or photocopy them.
2. Trace the patterns and assemble the pieces to make three large penguins.
3. Get three empty plastic containers. I used 24 ounce plastic cottage cheese containers or similar boxes. You can cover the containers with white paper to hide the label, if you wish.
4. Attach the penguins to the containers. I used Velcro® so that the penguins could be removed for easy storage, but you could glue them directly to the containers.
5. Reduce the patterns and assemble them to make one small penguin. It must be little enough to fit under the cottage cheese container.
6. Attach it to a Styrofoam cup either with glue or Velcro®.

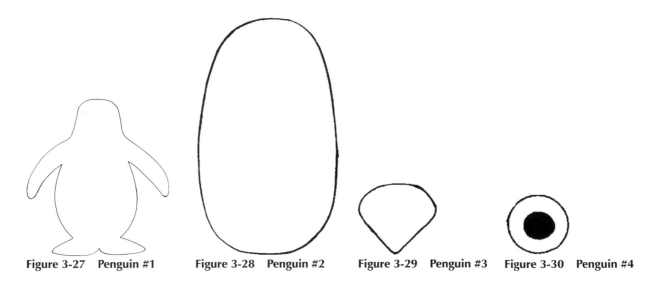

Figure 3-27  Penguin #1          Figure 3-28  Penguin #2          Figure 3-29  Penguin #3          Figure 3-30  Penguin #4

## 26. POSSUMS

**Words by Susan M. Dailey, Traditional Tune**                    **Possums (Animals)**

CD Track 52

### Song Presentation

Sing these words to the tune of "Twinkle, Twinkle, Little Star."

Make the visual aid, using the pattern provided on page 120.

Have the children move as indicated.

### Possums

Mr. Moon, what do you see?
  (*Point up, then put hand above eyes and look around.*)
Three little possums hanging in a tree.
  (*Hold up three fingers pointing down.*)

With shiny black eyes in the night
  (*Make small circle with fingers and hold up to eyes.*)
With whiskers and snouts of white
  (*Put hands away from face, then bring one hand forward and into point in front of nose.*)

Hairless tails and bodies gray
  (*Show "tail" and move hands from top of body to bottom.*)
But one little possum just ran away.
  (*Slap hands against legs quickly.*)

*End with:*

Mr. Moon, what do you see?
  (*Point up, then put hand above eyes and look around.*)
No little possums hanging in a tree.
  (*Shake head.*)

### Tips

- If you don't know this tune, "Twinkle, Twinkle, Little Star" can be found on *Early Childhood Classics: Old Favorites with a New Twist* by Hap Palmer.
- If you use a magnetic board, you can draw a tree branch on it to "hang" the possums on. With a flannel board, you could make one from felt.

### Picture Books to Pair with Song

Salley, Coleen. *Epossumondas*. Illustrated by Janet Stevens. Harcourt, 2002. A retelling of a classic tale in which a well-intentioned young possum continually takes his mother's instructions much too literally.
Van Laan, Nancy. *Possum Come a-Knockin'*. Illustrated by George Booth. Knopf, 1990. A cumulative tale in verse about a mysterious stranger who interrupts a family's daily routine.

### Patterns Needed

**Figure 3-31   Possum**

### Visual Aid Creation

1. See pattern above / CD file 3-31. Download and print the .pdf file or photocopy it.
2. Make three copies of the pattern, and color.
3. Put magnets on the back.

## 27. PUMPKINS, PUMPKINS

**Words by Susan M. Dailey, Traditional Tune**                    **Fall, Halloween**

CD Track 53

### Song Presentation

Sing these words to the tune of "Twinkle, Twinkle, Little Star."

Have the children move as indicated.

### Pumpkins, Pumpkins

Pumpkins, pumpkins on the ground
  (*Point to floor.*)
Pumpkins, pumpkins orange and round
  (*Make circle with arms.*)

Huge and tiny and in-between
  (*Show size with hands.*)
All want faces for Halloween
  (*Put hands up by face.*)

Smiling faces or maybe sad
  (*Make appropriate face.*)
Scary, silly or even mad

### Tips

- If you don't know this tune, "Twinkle, Twinkle, Little Star" can be found on *Early Childhood Classics: Old Favorites with a New Twist* by Hap Palmer.

### Picture Books to Pair with Song

Silverman, Erica. ***Big Pumpkin***. Illustrated by S.D. Schindler. Simon & Schuster, 1992. A witch trying to pick a big pumpkin on Halloween discovers the value of cooperation when she gets help from a series of monsters. (Halloween)

Spafford, Suzy. ***Fall is for Friends***. Illustrated by author. Scholastic, 2003. Suzy Ducken and her friend, Emily Marmot, love autumn because they like to jump into piles of dry leaves. But the leaves aren't falling from the trees, so the two girls try everything they can think of to encourage the leaves to fall. (Fall)

## 28. ROUND THE WORLD

**Words by Susan M. Dailey, Traditional Tune**                  **Vacations/Travel, Colors**

### Song Presentation

Sing these words to the tune of "The Farmer in the Dell."

This is a Name Tag Activity.

Make name tags according to the instructions below.

As you sing the song, have the children bring their name tags to you at the end of the appropriate verse.

### Round the World

We'll *travel* round the *world*
With *books* and crafts and *songs*.
If you have a passport green,
Now, please *come* along.

(*Continue with red, purple and blue.*)

### Tips

- If you don't know this tune, "The Farmer in the Dell" can be found on *Ultimate Kids Song Collection: 101 Favorite Sing-A-Longs* by the Wonder Kids Choir.
- Each week the children attended, I put a small stamp inside the booklet.
- Variation

  - I learned the sign language for the italicized words in the lyrics and taught it to the children. There are several websites that show sign language including *American Sign Language Browser* from Michigan State University. The address for this site is in Appendix 5. This site has video clips. There are also many wonderful sign language dictionaries. Two are listed in Appendix 5.
  - You could put magnets on the back of the passports and have the children put them on the board.

### Picture Book Pairings

Brown, Margaret Wise. *My World of Color.* Illustrated by Loretta Krupinski. Hyperion, 2002. Rhyming verses describe things that are red, orange, yellow, green, blue, purple, brown, black, gray, white, and pink. (Colors)

Priceman, Marjorie. *How to Make an Apple Pie and See the World.* Illustrated by author. Knopf, 1994. Since the market is closed, the reader is led around the world to gather the ingredients for making an apple pie. (World)

### Visual Aid Creation

1. To make the passports, cut construction paper into 4×6 inch rectangles in the various colors, and fold them to make a small booklet.
2. Write the childrens' names on the covers of their booklets. You can also write "Passport" on the covers.

## 29. SEASHELLS

**Words by Susan M. Dailey, Traditional Tune**                    **Sea, Beach, Summer**

### Song Presentation

Sing these words to the tune of "Twinkle, Twinkle, Little Star."

This is a Name Tag Activity.

Make name tags for each child, using the patterns below.

As you sing the song, have a few of the children bring their name tags to the magnetic/flannel board.

Count the number on the board. Sing the song again, filling in the correct number. I sang sample verses on the CD.

### Seashells

One little seashell
lying on the shore—
a wave rolls in
and then there are more.

### Tips

- If you don't know this tune, "Twinkle, Twinkle, Little Star" can be found on *Early Childhood Classics: Old Favorites with a New Twist* by Hap Palmer.

### Picture Book Pairings

Davis, Lambert. *Swimming with Dolphins.* Illustrated by author. Blue Sky Press, 2004. A young girl and her mother go to the beach, wait for the dolphins to arrive, then swim, glide, laugh, and swim with them until it is time to go home. Includes facts about dolphins and their encounters with people. (Sea)

Lakin, Patricia. *Beach Day.* Illustrated by Scott Nash. Dial, 2004. Four crocodile friends have many adventures on the way to the beach. (Summer)

Walvoord, Linda. *Razzamadaddy.* Illustrated by Sachiko Yoshikawa. Cavendish, 2004. A father and son spend a wonderful day together at the beach. (Beach)

### Patterns Needed

Figure 3-32   Seashell #1          Figure 3-33   Seashell #2

### Visual Aid Creation

1. See patterns above / CD files 3-32 and 3-33. Download and print .pdf files or photocopy them.
2. Copy the pattern and color them.
3. Put magnets on the back.

## 30. SHAKER

**Words by Susan M. Dailey, Traditional Tune**                    **Music, Opposites**

CD Track 54

### Song Presentation

Sing these words to the tune of "The Farmer in the Dell."

Make a simple shaker for each of the children out of two paper plates, using instructions below.

### Shaker

You shake your shaker high.
You shake your shaker low,
You shake your shaker fast, fast, fast,
and now you shake it slow.

You shake it to the left.
You shake it to the right.
You shake and shake your shake
until it's out of sight.

### Tips

- If you don't know this tune, "The Farmer in the Dell" can be found on *Ultimate Kids Song Collection: 101 Favorite Sing-A-Longs* by the Wonder Kids Choir.
- You could let the children decorate the shakers with stickers or markers as a craft project.
- Different seeds make different sounds. Experiment to get a good sound.
- Variations
    - We've also made shakers with pop cans or water bottles.

### Visual Aid Creation

*Paper Plate Shakers*

1. Place some corn kernels and other seeds between two plates.
2. Staple the sides together. You need to place the staples very close to each other so the seeds won't come out.

*Pop Can Shakers*

1. Place some corn kernels and other seeds inside.
2. Cover the hole with tape.
3. Wrap construction paper around the can.
4. Let the kids color on it or decorate it with stickers, if desired.
5. This kind of shaker shouldn't be used with toddlers or babies.

*Water Bottle Shakers*

1. Place some corn kernels and other seeds inside.
2. Wrap wide packing or duct tape around the lid so that the children can't open it.
3. You might want to use beads and sequins as well as seeds if you use clear bottles.

## Picture Book Pairings

Johnson, Angela. *Violet's Music.* Illustrated by Laura Huliska-Beith. Dial, 2004. From the days she banged her rattle in the crib, Violet has been looking for friends to share her love of music. (Music)

Milgrim, David. *My Friend Lucky.* Illustrated by author. Atheneum, 2002. A dog named Lucky demonstrates opposites such as slow and fast, dry and wet, cold and warm, and here and there. (Opposites)

## 31. SING A SONG OF STORYTIME

**Words by Susan M. Dailey, Traditional Tune**        **Libraries**

CD Track 55

### Song Presentation

Sing these words to the tune of "Sing a Song of Sixpence."
This is a Quiet Down Activity.

### Sing a Song of Storytime

Sing a song of storytime.
I'm so glad you're here!
Sing a song of storytime.
Let's all give a cheer!

With books and songs and fingerplays
We'll have lots of fun.
So get rid of your wiggles and sit very still,
'Cause storytime's begun.

### Tips

- If you don't know this tune, "Sing a Song of Sixpence" can be found on *Ultimate Kids Song Collection: 101 Favorite Sing-A-Longs* by the Wonder Kids Choir.
- You might want to pause to let the children wiggle during the second to last line. Then sing the rest of the song getting slower and quieter.

### Picture Book Pairings

Kimmel, Eric A. *I Took My Frog to the Library.* Illustrated by Blanche Sims. Viking Penguin, 1990. A young girl brings her pets to the library—with predictably disastrous results.

Numeroff, Laura Joffe. *Beatrice Doesn't Want To.* Illustrated by Lynn Munsinger. Candlewick, 2004. On the third afternoon of going to the library with her brother Henry, Beatrice finally finds something she enjoys doing.

## 32. SPRING IS HERE

**Words by Susan M. Dailey, Traditional Tune**                                                                 **Spring**

CD Track 56

### Song Presentation

Sing these words to the tune of "Frère Jacques."

Using the patterns on page 127, make visual aids for the song.

Have the children act out the motions indicated.

### Spring Is Here

I see flowers,
  (*Place one open hand on top of other palm, wiggle fingers.*)
I see birds' nests,
  (*Cup hand.*)
Butterflies,
  (*Touch palms with fingers pointing outward, move hands.*)
Rainy skies.
  (*Flutter fingers downward.*)
Everything is growing,
  (*Move hands upward.*)
The wind is gently blowing.
  (*Move hands back and forth in waving motion, and blow.*)
Spring is here!
Spring is here!

### Tips

- If you don't know this tune, "Frère Jacques" can be found on *Ultimate Kids Song Collection: 101 Favorite Sing-A-Longs* by the Wonder Kids Choir.

### Picture Book Pairings

Fowler, Allan. *How Do You Know It's Spring?* Illustrated by author. Children's Press, 1991. A simple description of the characteristics of spring.

Wilson, Karma. *Bear Wants More.* Illustrated by Jane Chapman. McElderry, 2003. When spring comes, Bear wakes up very hungry and is treated to great food by his friends.

**Patterns Needed**

**Figure 3-34    Bird Nest**

**Figure 3-35    Butterfly #2**

**Figure 3-36    Rain #2**

**Figure 3-37    Growing**

**Figure 3-38    Blowing**

## Visual Aid Creation

1. See patterns above / CD files 3-34 through 3-38. Download and print .pdf files or photo-copy them.
2. Use the pattern for flower from "Rainbow Farm" on page 55.
3. Color the patterns.
4. Put magnets on the back.

## 33. STARS

**Words by Susan M. Dailey, Traditional Tune**                                    **Moon & Stars**

### Song Presentation

Sing these words to the tune of "Twinkle, Twinkle Little Star."

This is a Name Tag Activity.

Make a name tag for each child using the pattern on page 128.

As you sing the song, have a few of the children bring their name tags to the magnetic/flannel board.

Count the number on the board. Sing the song again filling in the correct number.

### Stars

Twinkle, twinkle little star—
but we have just one so far.

We need more stars in the sky.
Bring yours up. Don't be shy.

If you bring your stars up here,
then we all can clap and cheer.

### Tips

• If you don't know this tune, "Twinkle, Twinkle, Little Star" can be found on *Early Childhood Classics: Old Favorites with a New Twist* by Hap Palmer.

### Picture Book Pairings

Harper, Cherise Mericle. ***There Was a Bold Lady Who Wanted a Star.*** Illustrated by author. Little, Brown, 2002. In this variation on the traditional cumulative rhyme, a feisty woman tries roller skates, a bicycle, and even a rocket to reach a star.

### Patterns Needed

**Figure 3-39   Star**

### Visual Aid Creation

1. See pattern above / CD file 3-39. Download and print the .pdf file or photocopy it.
2. Trace the pattern on construction paper.
3. Put magnets on the back.

## 34. SUMMER IS

**Words by Susan M. Dailey, Traditional Tune**                                    **Summer**

CD Track 57

### Song Presentation

Sing these words to the tune of "Johnny Pounds with One Hammer."
Have the children move as indicated.

### Summer Is

Summer is for fishing, fishing, fishing.
 (*Pretend to fish.*)
Summer is for fishing and baseball in the park.
 (*Pretend to hit ball.*)
Summer is for bare feet, bare feet, bare feet.
 (*Wiggle feet.*)
Summer is for bare feet and fireflies in the dark.
 (*Pretend to catch firefly.*)

Summer is for reading, reading, reading.
 (*Pretend to read.*)
Summer is for reading and swimming in the pool.
Even though the days are hot, days are hot, days are hot
 (*Fan yourself with hand.*)
Even though the days are hot, I think summer's cool!
 (*Hold up two thumbs.*)

### Tips

• If you don't know this tune, you could sing the lyrics to "Mary Wore her Red Dress," which
  can be found on *Raffi's Box of Sunshine* by Raffi.

### Picture Book Pairings

Fowler, Allan. *How Do You Know It's Summer?* Illustrated by author. Children's Press, 1992. Presents
  such signs of summer as heat, playtime, thunderstorms, growing, and fun.

## 35. TOOLBOX

**Words by Susan M. Dailey, Traditional Tune**                              **Construction**

CD Track 58

## Song Presentation

Sing these words to the tune of "This Old Man."

Make a visual aid using the patterns on page 131.

Have the children act out the words as indicated.

## Toolbox

Here's a box full of tools—
   (*Pretend to hold box.*)
A saw, a hammer and a wrench.
   (*Hold up 1, 2, 3 fingers.*)
Take the tools out of the box.
   (*Pretend to lift lid.*)
But first you have to unlock the lock.
   (*Pretend to turn key, make clicking sound with tongue.*)

Here's a saw that cuts through wood—
   (*Pretend to saw with hand on palm.*)
Back and forth and back and forth,
Back and forth and back and forth,
Back and forth and back and forth.

Here's a hammer that pounds in nails—
   (*Pound fists together.*)
Up and down and up and down,
Up and down and up and down,
Up and down and up and down.

Here's a wrench that tightens bolts—
   (*Pretend to hold wrench, move hand in circular motion.*)
Round and round and round and round,
Round and round and round and round,
Round and round and round and round.

Here's a box full of tools—
   (*Pretend to hold box.*)
A saw, a hammer and a wrench.
Put the tools back in the box.
   (*Pretend to close lid.*)
Then you have to relock the lock.
   (*Pretend to turn key, make clicking sound with tongue.*)

## Tips

• If you don't know this tune, "This Old Man" can be found on *Ultimate Kids Song Collection: 101 Favorite Sing-A-Longs* by the Wonder Kids Choir.

- I explained to the children that many toolboxes have locks for safety reasons or because they are left outside at construction sites.
- Variations

  - If you want to make this song more active, you can have the children stand up and move in the directions indicated in the song, i.e. back and forth, up and down, round and round.
  - You could make a toolbox for each of the children.

### Picture Book Pairings

Barton, Byron. **Building a House.** Illustrated by author. Greenwillow, 1981. Brief text and illustrations describe the steps in building a house.

Rockwell, Anne F. and Harlow Rockwell. **The Toolbox.** Illustrated by authors. Walker, 2004. An easy-to-read description of the basic tools found in a toolbox.

### Patterns Needed

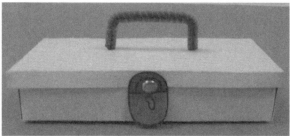

**Figure 3-40   Toolbox photo**

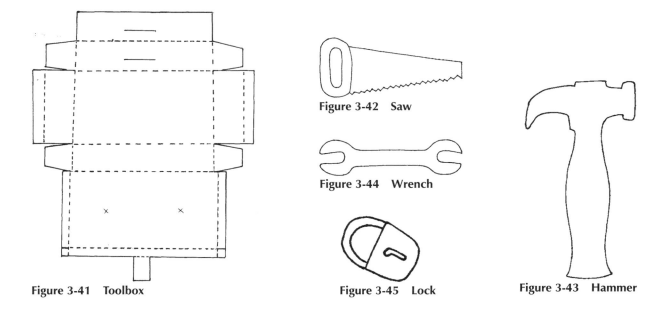

**Figure 3-41   Toolbox**

**Figure 3-42   Saw**

**Figure 3-44   Wrench**

**Figure 3-45   Lock**

**Figure 3-43   Hammer**

### Visual Aid Creation

1. See page 131 / CD files 3-41 through 3-45 for the pattern. Download and print .pdf files or photocopy them.
2. Enlarge the toolbox pattern.
3. Trace it on tagboard or poster board and cut out. I used manila colored tagboard, but you might want to use red or gray poster board.
4. Fold on the dotted lines. The front and sides of the "box" part have a double layer for stability. The sides have only a partial double layer to make the pattern fit on a standard 9" × 12" inch sheet of tagboard.
5. Note that the lid is slightly bigger than the "box" part so that it will close.
6. Glue the sides together.
7. Cut a slit through both layers of the front so the "latch" will slip inside.
8. Make a handle using a chenille stick. Bend each end and punch through the "X"s on the "lid." Bend the chenille sticks again and tape to the inside of the lid.
9. Trace the lock pattern on construction paper and attach to the lid with a paper fastener so it can be moved upward when it is "unlocked."
10. Trace the tool patterns on construction paper or tagboard and cut them out. You might want to laminate them. Place the tools inside the toolbox.

## 36. WASHING THE CAR

**Words by Susan M. Dailey, Traditional Tune**                    **Cars (Vehicles), Cleaning Up**

CD Track 59

### Song Presentation

Sing these words to the tune of "Mulberry Bush."
Have the children move as indicated.

### Washing the Car

Let's go out and wash the car
  (*Pretend to drive car.*)
Wash the car, wash the car.
Let's go out and wash the car
Because it is so dirty.

Take a brush and scrub the tires . . .
  (*Pretend to do motions as mentioned.*)
Because it is so dirty.

Take a sponge and soap the car . . .
Because they are so dirty.

Take a hose and rinse the car . . .
Because it is so soapy.

Take a towel and dry the car.
Now the car's not dirty.

### Tips

- This song can be found on *Early Childhood Classics: Old Favorites with a New Twist* by Hap Palmer.

### Picture Book Pairings

O'Garden, Irene. ***The Scrubbly-Bubbly Car Wash.*** Illustrated by Cynthia Jabar. HarperCollins, 2003. Rhythmic, rhyming text describes what happens as a car goes through a car wash. (Cars, Cleaning Up)

Teague, Mark. ***Pigsty.*** Illustrated by author. Scholastic, 1994. When Wendell doesn't clean up his room, a whole herd of pigs comes to live with him. (Cleaning Up)

Van Dusen, Chris. ***If I Built a Car.*** Illustrated by author. Dutton, 2005. Jack describes the kind of car he would build—one with amazing accessories and with the capability of traveling on land, in the air, and on and under the sea. (Cars)

## 37. WAVE YOUR RAINBOW

**Words by Susan M. Dailey, Traditional Tune**                    **Colors, Rain**

CD Track 60

### Song Presentation

Sing these words to the tune of "Yankee Doodle."

Make up visual aids for each of the children according to the directions below.

Have the children move as indicated.

**Wave Your Rainbow**

Red and orange and yellow and green,
  (*Have children point to appropriate color.*)
Then there's blue and purple.
Wave your rainbow, wave your rainbow,
  (*Move as indicated.*)
Wave your pretty rainbow.

Chorus:
Hold your rainbow way up high.
Wave your pretty rainbow.
Make it arc across the sky.
Yes, wave your pretty rainbow.
Wave your rainbow to one side.

Then wave it to the other.
Wave your rainbow up and down.
Yes, wave your pretty rainbow.

(*Repeat chorus.*)

Wave your rainbow fast, fast, fast.
Wave your rainbow slowly.
Wave it while you spin around.
Yes, wave your pretty rainbow.

(*Repeat chorus.*)

(*Repeat first verse.*)

## Tips

- If you don't know this tune, "Yankee Doodle" can be found on *Ultimate Kids Song Collection: 101 Favorite Sing-A-Longs* by the Wonder Kids Choir.
- Variation

  - For a craft, you could have the children decorate the visual aid themselves with stickers or markers.

## Picture Book Pairings

Kurtz, Jane. ***Rain Romp.*** Illustrated by Dyanna Wolcott. Greenwillow, 2002. When she awakens to a gray day, a little girl is in a grouchy mood until she and her parents find a way to make it better. (Rain)

Pinkney, Sandra L. ***A Rainbow All Around Me.*** Illustrated by Myles C. Pinkney. Scholastic, 2002. Photographs accompany the rhythmic text about colors seen every day. (Colors)

## Visual Aid Creation

1. Cut paper plate in quarters.
2. Tape a large craft stick to the point.
3. Tape streamers of the appropriate colors to the curved side.
4. I used ½ inch seam binding because it was inexpensive, but sturdy. You could use fabric ribbon, curling ribbon or crepe paper.
5. You might want to glue another quarter paper plate to the back to cover the tape and to give the prop more stability.
6. Decorate with stickers or markers.
7. Another prop that would work for this song is to make a paper chain with one loop of each color mentioned. Attach the chain to a large craft stick.

## 38. WE ARE GOING ON A BIKE RIDE

**Words by Susan M. Dailey, Traditional Tune**                    **Bicycles (Vehicles), Toys/Playing**

CD Track 61

### Song Presentation

Sing these words to the tune of "Reuben and Rachel."

Have the children roll their hands around each other during entire song.

### We Are Going on a Bike Ride

We are going on a bike ride.
Wheels on the bike go round and round.
Steer it straight and pedal steady,
But now look what we found . . .
Some potholes (*spoken*)
(*Dip hands quickly downward.*)

(*Sing verse again, but with the following at the end.*)

Bumps (*Move hands quickly upward.*)

Branches (*Move hands to side, as if swerves from branch.*)

Hill (*Move hands upward and slow the rolling motion of hands, then move downward and speed up rolling motion.*)

### Tips

- If you don't know this tune, "Reuben and Rachel" can be found on *Wee Sing Sing-Alongs* by the Pamela Conn Beale and Susan Hagen Nipp.
- The song "I Am Slowly Going Crazy" is sung to the same tune.

### Picture Book Pairings

Dubowski, Cathy East and Mark Dubowski. *Cowboy Roy.* Illustrated by author. Grosset, 2000. Roy, a young cowboy, tries hard to learn how to ride his bike without the training wheels. (Bicycles)

Steig, William. *Pete's a Pizza.* Illustrated by author. HarperCollins, 1998. When Pete feels miserable because rain makes it impossible to play ball outdoors, his father finds a fun indoor game to play with his son. (Toys/Playing)

## 39. YOU'RE MY FRIEND

**Words by Susan M. Dailey, Traditional Tune**                                        **Friends**

CD Track 62

### Song Presentation

Sing these words to the tune of "Three Blind Mice."

Learn the sign language for the italicized words and teach it to the children.

### You're My Friend

You're my *friend.*
You're my *friend.*
How do I *know*?
How do I *know*?
Because we like to *play together,*
because we like to *laugh together,*
because we like to *be together.*
You're my *friend.*
You're my *friend.*

### Tips

- If you don't know this tune, "Three Blind Mice" can be found on *Ultimate Kids Song Collection: 101 Favorite Sing-A-Longs* by the Wonder Kids Choir.
- There are several websites that show sign language including *American Sign Language Browser* from Michigan State University. The address for this site is in Appendix 5. This site has video clips. There are also many wonderful books with sign language. Two are listed in Appendix 5.

### Picture Book Pairings

Bloom, Suzanne. *A Splendid Friend, Indeed.* Illustrated by author. Boyds Mills Press, 2005. When a studious polar bear meets an inquisitive goose, they learn to be friends.

Polacco, Patricia. *Emma Kate.* Illustrated by author. Philomel, 2005. Emma Kate and her best friend, a toy elephant, share many activities, such as homework and soccer practice, and even have their tonsils out at the same time!

# CHAPTER 4

# TRADITIONAL SONGS, CAMP SONGS, AND CHANTS

**1. AIKEN DRUM**

**Traditional song**                                                                                   **Names, Food**

### Song Presentation

Make the visual aid using the patterns provided on pages 138–140.

Learn the song by finding it on the CD listed below.

As you sing the song, ask the children to pick one of the other foods on the board.

Put it where one of the eyes goes, and sing "One eye was made of . . ."

Continue adding other foods as the other parts of the face.

### Aiken Drum

There was a man lived in the moon,
in the moon, in the moon.
There was a man lived in the moon
and his name was Aiken Drum.

His hair was made of cotton candy,
cotton candy, cotton candy.
His hair was made of cotton candy
and his name was Aiken Drum.

### Tips

- A version of the song is available on *Singable Songs for the Very Young* by Raffi.
- Many versions contain a verse about playing on a ladle, but I omit this.

- Variations:
  - Instead of using the visual aid pattern draw an oval on flip chart paper or a marker board. As the children suggest foods for the various facial features, draw them in. (My limited artistic ability inspired me to make up this visual aid instead.)
  - Sometimes I let the children shout out what food they want chosen, and I pick one. With small groups that I know well, I'll call on specific children to choose a food.
  - We often sing the song more than once so that everyone can suggest a food.

## Picture Book Pairings

Capucilli, Alyssa Satin. ***Meet Biscuit!*** Illustrated by Pat Schories. HarperCollins, 2005. When the new puppy arrives, his young owner tries to decide on a name for it. Portions of this book were previously published as *Hello Biscuit!* (Names)

Goldstone, Bruce. ***The Beastly Feast.*** Illustrated by Blair Lent. Holt, 1998. All sorts of animals bring a variety of foods to share at a picnic: bears bring pears, parrots bring carrots, mosquitoes bring burritos, mice bring rice, and so on. (Food)

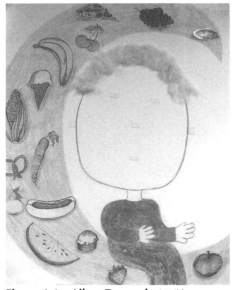

Figure 4-1   Aiken Drum photo #1

Figure 4-2   Aiken Drum photo #2

## Patterns Needed

Figure 4-3   Aiken Drum Pattern

Figure 4-4   Pizza

Figure 4-5   Apple

**Figure 4-6    Strawberry**

**Figure 4-7    Grapes**

**Figure 4-8    Cupcake**

**Figure 4-9    Ice Cream Cone**

**Figure 4-10    Cookie**

**Figure 4-11    Watermelon**

**Figure 4-12    Banana**

**Figure 4-13    Carrot**

**Figure 4-14    Pear**

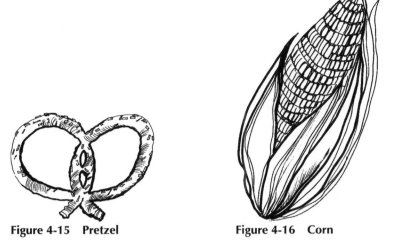

Figure 4-15   Pretzel

Figure 4-16   Corn

Figure 4-17   Candy

Figure 4-18   Hot Dog

Figure 4-19   Cherries

## Visual Aid Creation

1. Use an opaque projector to enlarge the Aiken Drum pattern on foam core board. Illustration board would also work. Both are stiff enough to be held on your lap. Poster board could be used, but you'd probably need to put it on an easel or in a poster frame.
2. Glue on colored cotton balls for the hair.
3. See pages 138–140 / CD files 4-3 through 4-19. Download and print .pdf files or photocopy them. Color the pieces.
4. Put the loop portion of the Velcro® on the food pieces.
5. Put a piece of the hook part of Velcro® where the eyes, nose, mouth and ears will go. Also put pieces of the hook portion around the moon.

## 2. ANTS GO MARCHING

**Traditional Song**                                                    **Bugs, Picnics**

### Song Presentation

Make the patterns on pages 142–143 to help the children remember the words.

Learn the song by finding it on the CD listed below.

As you sing the song, show the pictures as you get to each one in the song.

### Ants Go Marching

The ants go marching one by one,
Hurrah! Hurrah!
The ants go marching one by one,
Hurrah! Hurrah!
The ants go marching one by one.
The little one stops to suck his thumb
and they all go marching down to the ground
to get out of the rain.
Boom! Boom! Boom!

The ants go marching two by two . . .
The little one stops to tie his shoe . . .

The ants go marching three by three . . .
The litte one stops to climb a tree . . .

The ants go marching four by four . . .
The little one stops to slam a door . . .

The ants go marching five by five . . .
The little one stops and waves goodbye . . .

### Tips

- A version of the song can be found on *Ultimate Kids Song Collection: 101 Favorite Sing-A-Longs* by the Wonder Kids Choir.
- I use this shortened adaptation because the common version is long for preschoolers.
- I pause to let the children fill in the rhyme.
- Variations

  - Sometimes I hang all the graphics on a clothesline stretched across the room before we begin singing. I'll just point to them as we get to that part of the song.

## Picture Book Pairings

Jarrett, Clare. ***The Best Picnic Ever.*** Illustrated by author. Candlewick, 2004. While his mother prepares a picnic, Jack invites a giraffe, an elephant, and other animals to lunch and each eagerly agrees, as long as they can play first. (Picnics)

Sayre, April Pulley. ***Army Ant Parade.*** Illustrated by Rick Chrustowski. Holt, 2002. The reader experiences what happens when a swarm of army ants pass through the jungle. (Bugs)

## Patterns Needed

## Visual Aid Creation

1. See patterns below / CD files 4-20 through 4-29. Download and print .pdf files or photocopy them. Color the pieces.

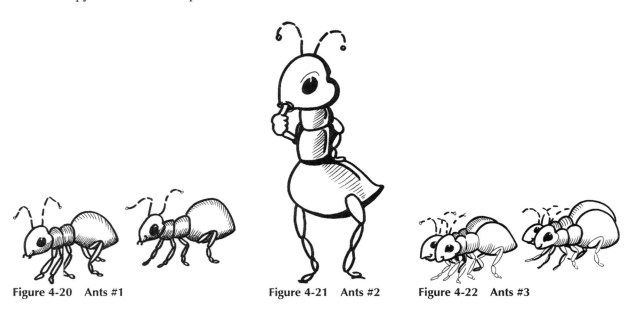

**Figure 4-20   Ants #1**          **Figure 4-21   Ants #2**          **Figure 4-22   Ants #3**

**Figure 4-23   Ants #4**

**Figure 4-24   Ants #5**

**Figure 4-25   Ants #6**

Figure 4-26    Ants #7

Figure 4-27    Ants #8

Figure 4-28    Ants #9

Figure 4-29    Ants #10

## 3. APPLESAUCE CHANT

**Words by Susan M. Dailey**                                    **Apples (Food), Fall**

### Song Presentation

This is a chant, not a song.

The chorus should be repeated between the verses.

Have the children move as indicated.

### Applesauce Chant

Chorus:
Apple, apple,
  (*Slap legs twice, then clap hands twice in rhythm.*)
Applesauce.
  (*Rub tummy in rhythm.*)

First you need apples,
so pick them, pick them (*Mimic picking.*)

Put them in the sink
and wash them, wash them (*Pretend to wash.*)

Then you take the apples
and cut them, cut them (*Make chopping action with one hand against other open palm.*)

Put them in a pot
and cook them, cook them (*Pretend to stir.*)

Pour them in a strainer
and squeeze them, squeeze them (*Squeeze hands together.*)

Take a little sugar
and sprinkle it, sprinkle it (*Pretend to sprinkle.*)

Then you take the sauce
and eat it, eat it (*Pretend to eat.*)

(*Repeat chorus several times at end—first at normal level, then quietly and finally loudly.*)

### Tips

- With young children, you might have them either clap their hands or slap their legs when you chant "apple, apple," instead of both.
- You can omit the motions on the chorus.

### Picture Book Pairings

Carr, Jan. ***Dappled Apples.*** Illustrated by Dorothy Donohue. Holiday House, 2001. Rhyming text and illustrations celebrate the pleasures of fall, from turning leaves and apple picking to pumpkins and Halloween. (Fall)

Hutchins, Pat. ***Ten Red Apples.*** Illustrated by author. Greenwillow, 2000. In rhyming verses, one animal after another neighs, moos, oinks, quacks and makes other appropriate sounds as each eats an apple from the farmer's tree. (Apples)

## 4. BINGO

**Traditional song**                                          **Dogs (Animals), Names, Farms**

### Song Presentation

Make the visual aid using the patterns provided on page 146.

Place the letters on a magnetic or flannel board.

On each verse, replace one letter with a bark.

Cover up the letter with a picture of a dog.

**Bingo**

There was a farmer had a dog
and Bingo was his name-o.
B-I-N-G-O, B-I-N-G-O, B-I-N-G-O
and Bingo was his name-o.

There was a farmer had a dog
And Bingo was his name-o.
Woof-I-N-G-O, Woof-I-N-G-O, Woof-I-N-G-O
and Bingo was his name-o.

*(Continue replacing other letters by saying "woof.")*
*—idea from Meggan Conway, Lexington Public Library*

**Tips**

- A version of this song can also be found on *Early Childhood Classics: Old Favorites with a New Twist* by Hap Palmer.
- Variation

  - I learned to sing this song by replacing each letter with a clap; however, young children have difficulty doing this. Megan Conway recommended this alternative at a conference and it works terrifically. She also suggested the visual aid.

**Picture Book Pairings**

McFarland, Lyn Rossiter. *Widget.* Illustrated by author. Farrar, 2001. A small stray dog is accepted into a household full of cats by learning to "fit in," but when his mistress is hurt, he demonstrates that being a dog is not all bad. (Dogs)

Mosel, Arlene. *Tikki Tikki Tembo.* Illustrated by Blair Lent. Holt, 1989. When the eldest son fell in the well and most of the time getting help was spent pronouncing the name of the one in trouble, the Chinese, according to legend, decided to give all their children short names. (Names)

Rostoker-Gruber, Karen. *Rooster Can't Cock-a-Doodle-Doo.* Illustrated by Paul Rátz de Tagyos. Dial, 2004. When Rooster's throat is too sore for him to crow, the other farm animals help both him and Farmer Ted. (Farms)

**Figure 4-30   Bingo photo #1**

**Figure 4-31   Bingo photo #2**

## Patterns Needed

Figure 4-32    Bingo

Figure 4-33    Bingo-B

Figure 4-34    Bingo-I

Figure 4-35    Bingo-N

Figure 4-36    Bingo-G

Figure 4-37    Bingo-O

## Visual Aid Creation

1. See patterns above / CD files 4-32 through 4-37. Download and print .pdf files or photocopy them.
2. Make five cards with a dog on each.
3. Color the pieces.

## 5. CRAZY CHANT

**Words by Susan M. Dailey**                    **Nonsense, Books/Libraries**

### Song Presentation

This is a chant, not a song.

You can clap along or alternate slapping your thighs and clapping your hands in a rhythmic beat.

Say the rhyme several times, doing it in different ways, e.g. loudly, softly, slowly, fast.

It's also fun to do it in a high-pitched voice.

### Crazy Chant

Hickory dickory dock,
E-I-E-I-O,
Hey diddle diddle,
Eeny meeny miny moe,

Diddle diddle dumpling,
Fee fie foe fum,
Rub-a-dub-dub—
all sound kind of dumb!

What do they mean?
Who can say?
But they're fun to chant
this-a-way!

### Tips

- This chant can be challenging so I'd reserve it for older preschoolers or even elementary students.

### Picture Book Pairings

Bruss, Deborah. *Book! Book! Book!* Illustrated by Tiphanie Beeke. Arthur A. Levine Books, 2001. When the children go back to school, the animals on the farm are bored, so they go into the library in town trying to find something to do. (Books/Libraries)

Grossman, Bill. *My Little Sister Ate One Hare.* Illustrated by Kevin Hawkes. Crown, 1996. Little sister has no problem eating one hare, two snakes, and three ants, but when she gets to ten peas, she throws up quite a mess. (Nonsense)

## 6. DOWN ON GRANDPA'S FARM

**Traditional song**                                    **Farms, Sounds, Grandparents (Families)**

### Song Presentation

Make the visual aid, using the patterns provided on pages 149 and 173.

Add the animals to the barn on the appropriate verse.

Learn the song by finding it on the CD listed below.

### Down on Grandpa's Farm

Chorus:
We're on our way, we're on our way,
on the way to Grandpa's farm.
We're on our way, we're on our way,
on the way to Grandpa's farm.

Down on Grandpa's farm there is a big brown cow.
Down on Grandpa's farm there is a big brown cow.
The cow, she makes a sound like this . . . Moo!
The cow, she makes a sound like this . . . Moo!

Down on Grandpa's farm there is a big pink pig . . .

Down on Grandpa's farm, there is a little white sheep . . .

Down on Grandpa's farm, there is a little brown rooster . . .

Down on Grandpa's farm, there is a big black dog . . .

Down on Grandpa's farm, there is a little yellow cat . . .

### Tips

- A version of this song can be found on *Raffi's Box of Sunshine* by Raffi.
- You can slap your hands on your thighs or clap your hands on the chorus.
- Variation

  - Make enough barns for each child to have one to use while you sing the song.
  - Have the children remove the animals before you start singing the song and then add them on the appropriate verse.

- This prop could also be used with "Old MacDonald Had a Farm."

### Picture Book Pairings

Ackerman, Karen. *Song and Dance Man.* Illustrated by Stephen Gammell. Grandpa demonstrates for his visiting grandchildren some of the songs, dances, and jokes he performed when he was a vaudeville entertainer. (Grandparents)

Hindley, Judy. *Does a Cow Say Boo?* Illustrated by Brita Granström. Candlewick, 2002. Children on a farm want to know which creature says "boo," and learn about animal sounds as they search. (Farms, Sounds)

## Patterns Needed

Figure 4-38    Barn photo

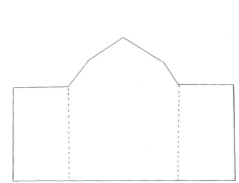

Figure 4-39    Barn

Figure 4-40    Cow #1

Figure 4-41    Sheep #1

Figure 4-42    Rooster

Figure 4-43    Cat #1

Figure 4-44    Dog #2

## Visual Aid Creation

1. See patterns above / CD files 4-39 through 4-44. Download and print .pdf files or photocopy them.
2. Enlarge the pattern for the barn to fit a large sheet of red construction paper or poster board.
3. Fold in the sides to create doors.
4. Add strips of white paper for the windows, doors and roof features.
5. Copy the animal patterns on the correct color of construction paper or color them.
6. Use the hog from "Little Red Hen" on page 173 for the pig.
7. Attach Velcro® to the back of the animals and to the inside of the barn.
8. You might want to laminate the pieces before attaching the Velcro®.

## 7. FIVE GREEN APPLES

**Traditional song**                                           **Apples (Food), Fall, Farms**

### Song Presentation

Make the visual aid, using the patterns provided on page 151.

Begin the song with five apples on the tree.

Remove one apple at the end of each verse.

Replace it with an apple core at the bottom of the board.

Make sure to leave the apple with the worm for the last verse.

Learn the song by finding it on the CD listed below.

### Five Green Apples

Farmer Brown had five green apples
hanging on his tree.
Farmer Brown had five green apples
hanging on his tree.
And he plucked one apple
  (*Remove apple from tree.*)
and ate it hungrily,
  (*Pretend to eat, place core on bottom of board.*)
leaving four green apples
hanging on his tree.

(*Repeat with four, three, two and one.*)

Last verse:
Farmer Brown had one green apple
hanging on his tree.
Farmer Brown had one green apple
hanging on his tree.
And he plucked that apple
and gave it just to me.
  (*Turn apple over and show worm on back.*)
Yuch! (spoken)
Leaving no green apples
hanging on his tree.

### Tips

- A version of this song can be found on *Mainly Mother Goose* by Sharon, Lois and Bram.
- In 2001, Weston Woods produced a wonderful video of ***Click, Clack, Moo: Cows that Type***.

### Picture Book Pairings

Cronin, Doreen. ***Click, Clack, Moo: Cows that Type.*** Illustrated by Betsy Lewin. Simon & Schuster, 2000. When Farmer Brown's cows find a typewriter in the barn they start making demands, and go on strike when the farmer refuses to give them what they want. (Farms)

Kelley, Marty. ***Fall Is Not Easy.*** Illustrated by author. Zino Press Children's Books, 1998. A tree tells why, out of all four seasons, autumn is the hardest. (Fall)

Wellington, Monica. ***Apple Farmer Annie.*** Illustrated by author. Dutton, 2001. Annie the apple farmer saves her most beautiful apples to sell fresh at the farmers' market. (Apples)

**Figure 4-45   Apple Tree photo**

### Patterns Needed

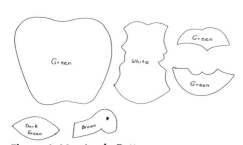

**Figure 4-46   Apple Patterns**

### Visual Aid Creation

1. See patterns above / CD file 4-46. Download and print .pdf files or photocopy them.
2. Using the patterns, cut five green apples out of construction paper.
3. On the back side of one apple, glue a worm also cut from construction paper.
4. In addition, make four apple cores. You can laminate the apples and cores.
5. Draw a tree on a piece of foam core board.
6. Put five pieces of Velcro® on the leafy part of the tree for the apples and four pieces at the bottom of the tree for the cores.

## 8. I LIKE MY BIKE CHANT

**Words by Susan M. Dailey**                    **Bicycles (Vehicles), Toys/Playing**

### Song Presentation

This is a chant, not a song.

Say a line and have the children repeat it.

The chorus should be repeated between each two verses.

### My Bike Chant

Chorus:
My bike, my bike,
I like my bike.

Verses:
It has two wheels
and is bright green—
the neatest bike
I've ever seen.

It has three gears
and handlebars.
I ride it near.
I ride it far.

It has a bell
That goes brrrng, brrrng. (*Roll tongue.*)
I'd not trade it
for anything.

### Tips

• End by repeating the chorus several times, getting softer and softer.

### Picture Book Pairings

Wong, Janet S. *Hide & Seek.* Illustrated by Margaret Chodos-Irvine. Harcourt, 2005. In this counting
    book, a child and parent play hide-and-seek while they bake cookies. (Toys/Playing)
Shannon, David. *Duck on a Bike.* Illustrated by author. Scholastic, 2002. A duck decides to ride a bike
    and soon influences all the other animals on the farm to ride bikes too. (Bicycles)

## 9. MAGALENA HAGALENA

**Camp Song**                                                                          **Names, Nonsense**

### Song Presentation

Make the visual aid using the pattern provided on page 154.

Teach the children the chorus by breaking it into short segments.

Point to the various body parts as you sing the song.

### Magalena Hagalena

Chorus:
Magalena Hagalena Ook-a Talk-a Walk-a Talk-a
O-ka Po-ka No-ka was her name.

She had two hairs on the top of her head.
One was green and the other one was red.

She had two eyes on the middle of her face.
One rolled around while the other stayed in place.

She had two teeth in the middle of her mouth.
One pointed north while the other pointed south.

She had two arms in the middle of her chest.
One was naked while the other one was dressed.

She had two legs at the bottom of her body.
One was plain while the other one was spotty.

She had two feet at the bottom of her legs.
One was pink like ham, the other white like eggs.

### Tips

- There are many versions of this character's name. You can find others in the book by Tedd Arnold.
- I changed some of the verses so that they could be depicted on the visual aid.

### Picture Book Pairings

Arnold, Tedd. *Catalina Magdalena Hoopensteiner Wallendiner Hogan Logan Bogan Was Her Name.* Illustrated by author. Scholastic, 2004. Pre-

**Figure 4-47  Magalena Hagalena photo**

sents the original tune–and varying forms of the name–of a classic camp song that dates at least from the 1940s. (Names, Nonsense)

Weeks, Sarah. *Mrs. McNosh Hangs up the Wash.* Illustrated by Nadine Bernard Westcott. Harper-Collins, 1998. Mrs. McNosh hangs up her wash with such gusto that her clothesline ends up holding the dog, a Christmas wreath, a kite, and other odd items. (Nonsense)

**Patterns Needed**

**Figure 4-48   Magalena Hagalena Pattern**

## Visual Aid Creation

1. See pattern above / CD file 4-48. Download and print the .pdf file or photocopy it.
2. Enlarge it so that it fits on illustration board, which I use because it is sturdier. However, poster board would also work.
3. The two hairs were made with a green and red chenille stick that was taped to the board.
4. I used yarn for the rest of the hair.
5. For the eye that rolled around, I bought a "frog" eye at a craft store. This kind of eye has a shank, which I poked through the board. I could make the eye roll by turning the shank.
6. The spots on the legs were made with ¼" colored self-adhesive dots purchased at an office supply store.
7. I glued fabric to the board for her shirt and skirt.

# CHAPTER 5

# STORIES THAT SING!

## OVERVIEW

"Folktales with singing interludes are common in many cultures," Margaret Read MacDonald states in her book *Shake-it-up Tales!* (MacDonald, 2000: 31). She notes that song serves three purposes in African and Caribbean storytelling. It allows the audience to participate and rests the teller. Furthermore, song is used to expand the story. Some European tales also include musical refrains. Great Britain and Appalachia are both sources of many folktales told entirely in song (MacDonald, 2000).

In 1955, John Langstaff wrote *Frog Went a-Courtin'*, which recounts the story of a frog and mouse's romance as told in an American folk song. The book, which was illustrated by Feodor Rojankovsky, remains in print more than 50 years later. Recently Mary Ann Hoberman, Iza Trapani and Will Hillenbrand have written expanded versions of common folk songs. The appendix contains a bibliography of "singable" picture books.

As with the songs in the previous section, I've suggested themes and picture books to pair with each original story in this chapter. There are suggested tips and illustrations to help use the stories.

## REFERENCE

MacDonald, Margaret Read. *Shake-it-up Tales! Stories to Sing, Dance, Drum, and Act Out*. August House, 2000.

## STORIES WITH MUSICAL REFRAINS

In *Lizard's Song*, George Shannon relates the story of a greedy bear that wants lizard's wonderful song. It's an obvious decision to sing the refrain in this story. A melody is even provided. However, a simple tune could be added to the Gingerbread Man's repeated boasts. The four stories in this section all include repetitive phrases that are musical. "Beautiful Monkey" and "Bunny Hop Hop" include musical refrains set to common tunes. "Nobody Loves Me" uses a slightly altered version of the childhood song. The musical refrain in "Joey Goes Fishing" is set to an original tune.

## 1. BEAUTIFUL MONKEY

**The refrain is sung to "Oh, Dear! What Can the Matter Be?"**

**Suggested themes: Monkeys (Animals), Zoo**

## Pieces Needed

- Monkey
- Monkey's mama
- Thought bubble with monkey with zebra stripes
- Thought bubble with monkey with tiger stripes
- Thought bubble with monkey with leopard spots
- Thought bubble with monkey with giraffe spots
- Thought bubble with monkey colored brightly like parrot

High in the tree on Monkey Island, Little Monkey just sat and stared at the zoo below. (*Put monkey on board.*) His momma swung over to him. (*Put monkey's mama on board.*) "What's wrong?" she asked.

Little Monkey sighed and told his momma that he'd heard a teacher say to a group of students, "There are so many beautiful animals at the zoo with stripes or spots or gorgeous colors. I can't wait to show them to you."

Little Monkey looked down at his plain brown hair and sighed again. Then he sang:

Oh, I wish I were beautiful.
Oh, I wish I were beautiful.
I could be very beautiful
If I had stripes like zebra.

Little Monkey and his momma imagined what he would look like with zebra stripes. (*Put appropriate thought bubble on board.*) "Wouldn't I be beautiful?" Little Monkey asked his momma.

"I already think you are beautiful," said Momma. "In fact, I think you'd look rather funny with zebra stripes. But funny is good, too."

"No, I don't want to look funny," said Little Monkey. "I want to look beautiful."

Little Monkey looked around the zoo and saw the area where the big cats lived. Then he sang:

Oh, I wish I were beautiful.
Oh, I wish I were beautiful.
I could be very beautiful
If I had stripes like tiger.

He and his momma imagined what he would look like. (*Put appropriate thought bubble on board.*) "Don't you think I'd be beautiful with tiger stripes?" Little Monkey asked his momma.

"I love you just the way you are," said Momma. "In fact, I think you'd look rather funny with tiger stripes. But funny is good, too."

"Not funny . . . beautiful," said Little Monkey. "Maybe I would look beautiful with spots instead of stripes." Then he sang:

Oh, I wish I were beautiful.
Oh, I wish I were beautiful.
I could be very beautiful
If I had spots like leopard.

He and his momma imagined what he would look like with leopard spots. (*Put appropriate thought bubble on board.*) "That would make me beautiful," said Little Monkey.

"You are wonderful just the way you are," said Momma. "In fact, I think you'd look rather funny with leopard spots. But funny is good, too."

"I want to look beautiful," said Little Monkey. Then he sang:

Oh, I wish I were beautiful.
Oh, I wish I were beautiful.
I could be very beautiful
If I had spots like giraffe.

He and his momma imagined what he would look like. (*Put appropriate thought bubble on board.*) "Don't you think I'd be beautiful with giraffe spots?" Little Monkey asked his momma.

"I think you are already beautiful," said Momma. "In fact, I think you'd look rather funny with giraffe spots. But funny is good, too."

"Who likes funny?" said Little Monkey angrily. "I want to be beautiful!"

He looked around the zoo at all the other animals. Then he sang:

Oh, I wish I were beautiful.
Oh, I wish I were beautiful.
I could be very beautiful
If I had colors like parrot.

He and his momma imagined what he would look like. (*Put appropriate thought bubble on board.*) "I know I'd be beautiful with parrot's colors."

"Little Monkey, you are perfect just the way you are. And in fact, you'd look rather funny with feathers. But funny is good, too."

"Not funny! Beautiful!" Little Monkey shouted. "Nobody likes funny."

Just then, Little Monkey and his momma heard a girl say, "Teacher, teacher, let's go look at the monkeys. They are so funny. I love them!"

Little Monkey stared down at the many, many people watching the monkeys. They were smiling and laughing.

Little Monkey smiled, too. "Funny *is* good!" he said to his momma. Then Little Monkey went chitter-chattering and swinging happily through the trees.

### Tips

- If you don't know the tune, "Oh, Dear! What Can the Matter Be?" can be found on *Mainly Mother Goose* by Sharon, Lois and Bram.
- Photocopy and color the visuals provided to make the pieces. Teach the children the refrain before you start the story.

### Picture Book Pairings

De Regniers, Beatrice Schenk. *May I Bring a Friend?* Illustrated by Beni Montresor. Atheneum, 1964. A well-mannered little boy has permission to bring his animal friends to visit the king and queen. (Zoos)

Slobodkina, Esphyr. *Caps for Sale*. Illustrated by author. HarperCollins, 1984. A band of mischievous monkeys steals every one of a peddler's caps while he takes a nap under a tree. (Monkeys)

**Figure 5-1   Monkey**

**Figure 5-2   Monkey's Mama**

**Figure 5-3   Monkey with Zebra Stripes**

**Figure 5-4   Monkey with Tiger Stripes**

**Figure 5-5   Monkey with Leopard Spots**

**Figure 5-6   Monkey with Giraffe Spots**

**Figure 5-7   Monkey with Parrot Colors**

## 2. BUNNY HOP HOP

**The refrain is sung to "Pop Goes the Weasel"**          **Suggested themes: Rabbits, Movement, Senses**

### Pieces Needed

- Rabbit
- Clover
- Lawn Mower
- Apple Tree with detachable apples
- Dog
- Cat
- Carrots
- Lap Stage

Bunny dreamed of carrots. (Hold up bunny.) He dreamed about how delicious they tasted—how wonderful they looked and smelled and even felt and sounded as he ate them. But Bunny didn't have any carrots . . . so he went searching for some.

Bunny hopped and hopped for a long time. Then he saw some . . . *clover*. (Put up clover.) Now, clover isn't carrots, but it would have to do, because Bunny was very hungry. He hopped over to the clover and began to nibble. Suddenly, he stopped and listened. He heard (droning sound). (Remove clover, put up lawn mower.) It was a lawn mower coming right toward him!

Hop, bunny, you'd better hop.
Hop, hop, hop, hop, hop, hop,
Hop, hop, hop, hop, hop, hop, hop, hop.
Now you can stop! (remove lawn mower)

Bunny slipped under a fence and into an apple orchard. (Put up apple tree.) Bunny stopped to rest under a tree. He felt the wind blow. It blew hard and then harder. Suddenly, an apple crashed to the ground. (Remove apples from tree.) He felt it hit right beside his paw. Then another apple hit him, on the tail. Apples rained from the trees, smashing the ground.

Hop, bunny, you'd better hop.
Hop, hop, hop, hop, hop, hop,
Hop, hop, hop, hop, hop, hop, hop, hop.
Now you can stop! (Remove apple tree.)

Bunny saw . . . some more clover. (Put up clover again) Now, clover isn't carrots, but it would have to do, because Bunny was very, very hungry. He hopped over and began to nibble. Suddenly, he stopped and looked. He saw a dog running right toward him. (Remove clover, put up dog.)

Hop, bunny, you'd better hop.
Hop, hop, hop, hop, hop, hop,
Hop, hop, hop, hop, hop, hop, hop, hop.
Now you can stop! (Remove dog.)

Bunny hopped into a barn. Bunny couldn't see anything. It was dark in the barn. He couldn't hear anything. It was quiet in the barn. He couldn't feel anything, but . . . Bunny twitched his nose. He smelled something! (Put up cat.) It smelled like *cat*, and the smell was getting stronger. The cat was coming toward him!

Hop, bunny, you'd better hop.
Hop, hop, hop, hop, hop, hop,
Hop, hop, hop, hop, hop, hop, hop, hop.
Now you can stop! (Remove cat.)

Suddenly Bunny saw something. It was . . . carrots! (Put up carrots.) Bunny hopped over and nibbled the carrots. They tasted just as delicious as Bunny had dreamed they would!

## Tips

- If you don't know this tune, "Pop Goes the Weasel" can be found on *Ultimate Kids Song Collection: 101 Favorite Sing-A-Longs* by the Wonder Kids Choir.
- This story works better as a puppet show than as a magnetic/flannel board story because you can make the bunny hop more easily. Photocopy and color the visuals to make the patterns. Use the dog from "Bingo" on page 146 and carrot from "Aiken Drum" on page 139. Attach the pieces to craft sticks. Note that the bunny needs to be two-sided so that he can hop in both directions. If you want to fashion a lap stage, the instructions are in the appendix.
- Sometimes I give the children a bunny puppet and have them make their bunny hop. Other times I encourage the children to use their hands, by holding up two fingers in a "V" shape and "hopping" them.

## Picture Book Pairings

Bruel, Nick. *Boing!* Illustrated by author. Roaring Brook, 2004. A mother kangaroo and various woodland animals coach her joey as the little one attempts her first jump. (Movement)

Fleming, Candace. *Muncha! Muncha! Muncha!* Illustrated by G. Brian Karas. Atheneum, 2002. After planting the garden he has dreamed of for years, Mr. McGreely tries to find a way to keep some persistent bunnies from eating all his vegetables. (Rabbits)

Ryan, Pam Muñoz. *Hello Ocean*. Illustrated by Mark Astrella. Charlesbridge, 2001. Using rhyming text, a child describes the wonder of the ocean experienced through each of her five senses. (Senses)

Figure 5-8    Rabbit #1

Figure 5-9    Rabbit #2

Figure 5-10    Clover

Figure 5-11    Lawn Mower

Figure 5-12    Apple Tree

Figure 5-13    Cat #4

## 3. JOEY GOES FISHING

**The refrain is an original tune.**                    **Suggested themes: Fish, Brothers (Family)**

### Pieces Needed

- Joey
- Jake, Jack and Jeff
- Jimmy, looking forward
- Mom #1
- Jimmy, with fishing pole and fish
- Jeff, facing sideways
- Jack, facing sideways
- Jake, facing sideways
- Fish

(Put up Joey.) Joey's brothers were going fishing. "Can I come fishing, too?" he asked.

"No," said Jake, Jack and Jeff. (Put up three boys.)

"No way!" said Jimmy. (Put up Jimmy, looking forward.)

"Boys, please take Joey with you," said their mom. (Put up Mom.)

"He's too little," said Jake. "He won't be able to keep up on his bike."

"He's too little," said Jack. "He won't be able to bait his own hook."

"He's too little," said Jeff. "He won't be able to cast his line without getting it tangled."

"He's just a baby," said Jimmy. "He won't be able to pull in his own fish—even if it's teeny tiny!"

"I'm not a baby!" said Joey. "I'm almost as old as you are, Jimmy!"

"It would be really nice for you to take Joey along," said Mom.

"O.K.," said Jake, Jack, Jeff and Jimmy.

So the boys grabbed their poles and headed to the pond. And Joey couldn't keep up on his bike. Jake had to keep stopping to wait for Joey.

And Joey couldn't bait his own hook. Jack had to bait it.

And Joey couldn't cast his own line without getting it tangled. Jeff had to cast it. (Take down three boys.)

And Joey didn't catch anything—not even a teeny tiny fish. But Jimmy did. (Take down Jimmy piece, replace with Jimmy with fishing pole.)

So he pulled on the pole.
and he pulled on the pole.
And he pulled, pulled, pulled on the pole, pole, pole,
but he couldn't land that fish.

"I caught a big fish!" said Jimmy.

"I can help," said Joey.

"You're too little," said Joey. "Go get Jeff."

So Joey got Jeff. (Put up Jeff.) Jeff pulled on Jimmy while. . . .

So he pulled on the pole.
And he pulled on the pole.
And he pulled, pulled, pulled on the pole, pole, pole,
but he couldn't land that fish.

"I caught a huge fish!" said Jimmy.
"I can help," said Joey.
"You're too little," said Joey. "Go get Jack."
So Joey got Jack. (Put up Jack.) Jack pulled on Jeff. Jeff pulled on Jimmy while . . .

So he pulled on the pole.
And he pulled on the pole.
And he pulled, pulled, pulled on the pole, pole, pole,
but he couldn't land that fish.

"I caught a giant fish!" said Jimmy.
"I can help," said Joey.
"You're too little," said Joey. "Go get Jake."
So Joey got Jake. (Put up Jake.) Jake pulled on Jack. Jack pulled on Jeff. Jeff pulled on Jimmy while . . .

So he pulled on the pole.
And he pulled on the pole.
And he pulled, pulled, pulled on the pole, pole, pole,
but he couldn't land that fish.

"I caught a gigantic fish!" said Jimmy.
"I can help," said Joey.
"Well, O.K.," said Jimmy.
Joey waded into the water. He reached down and untangled the fishing line from the branch that it was caught on. Then he pulled up the fish. (Reveal fish.)
"You did catch a gigantic fish," Joey said, "But I helped!"

## Tips

- See page 166 for sheet music.
- Encourage the children to sing the refrain with you and to pretend to pull on a pole as they sing it.
- This variation of "The Turnip" story works as a puppet show. Photocopy and color the visuals to make the patterns. Use "Something's Hiding in a Flower" on page 64. Attach the fish to the fishing pole using fishing line. Make sure the line is long enough so that the fish can be hidden below the stage. Attach them to craft sticks. If you want to fashion a lap stage, the instructions are on page 165.
- I've used props to tell the story instead of puppets. I created the pole with a 1/4 inch dowel rod, some fishing line and a paper clip. Then I made a large fish and punched a hole in it,

which I hooked to the paper clip. I wrapped the fishing line around a small tree branch and hid everything under a blue towel.

- During the first part, I simply told the story. When Jimmy caught the fish, I reached down and picked up the fishing pole. I pulled on it hard enough to make the dowel rod bend. I put my foot on the towel to keep it from coming up when I pulled on the rod. When Joey wades into the water, I showed the children the branch and unwrapped the line. Then I revealed the fish.

### Picture Book Pairings

Curtis, Marci. **Big Brother, Little Brother**. Illustrated by author. Dial, 2004. Photographs and rhyming text show the ups and downs of having a big or little brother. (Brothers)

Martin, David. **Piggy and Dad Go Fishing**. Illustrated by Frank Remkiewicz. Candlewick, 2005. When his dad takes Piggy fishing for the first time and Piggy ends up feeling sorry for the worms and the fish, they decide to make some changes. (Fish)

Figure 5-14  Joey          Figure 5-15  Three Brothers          Figure 5-16  Jimmy #1

**Figure 5-17   Mom #1**

**Figure 5-18   Jimmy #2**

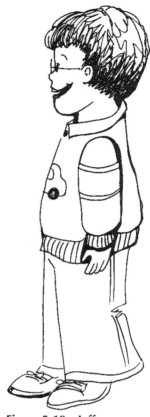

**Figure 5-19   Jeff**

**Figure 5-20   Jake**

**Figure 5-21   Jack**

Instructions for Making a Lap Stage

1. Get a corrugated cardboard box approximately 18 inches long, 10 inches wide and at least 4 inches high.  The length determines the stage length.  The width determines how high the top of the stage will be from your lap.  The height determines how much space the stage will have to store props out of sight.  See diagram #1.
2. Fold the small side flaps in.  Then tape one of the large flaps closed.  See diagram #2.
3. Cut off the remaining large flap.  See diagram #3.
4. Cut off the area of the side flaps that are visible above the taped flap.  See diagram #4.
5. Draw a diagonal line from the top of the taped flap to the opposite corner on each side.  See diagram #5.
6. Cut this side area and the top away.  See diagram #6.
7. Cover the box with Con-Tact® paper.
8. Double stick foam tape can be placed along the inner top edge.  Props can be secured here during the story.  Leave the liner on the tape unless it is being used.  This will prevent the tape from losing its stickiness.

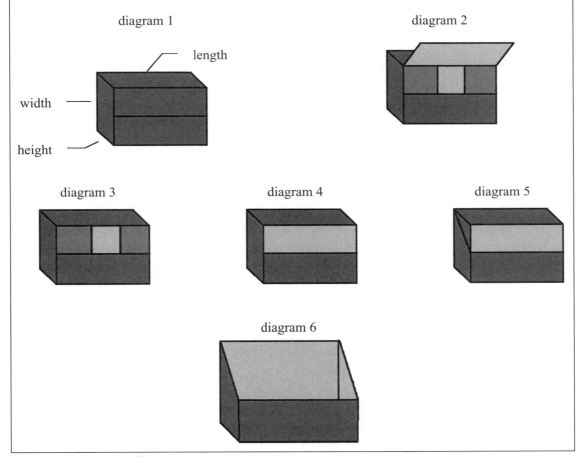

**Figure 5-22    Lap Stage directions**

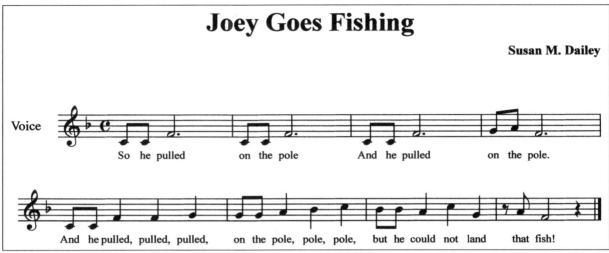

**Figure 5-23   Joey Goes Fishing sheet music**

## 4. NOBODY LOVES ME

**The refrain in this story is sung to "Nobody Likes Me."**

Suggested themes: Families, Love, Valentine's Day

### Pieces Needed

- Nicky
- Mom #2
- Dad
- Grandpa
- Grandma
- Sarah
- Bart
- Dog

Nicky lived in a house overflowing with family. (Put up pieces as they are mentioned.) There were his mom and dad, Grandpa and Grandma, his "a lot older sister," Sarah, and his "little bit older" brother, Bart. There was even his dog, Digby. (Remove all pieces except Nicky and Bart.)

One day, he asked Bart to play with him.

"Nope," said Bart. (Remove Bart, put up Mom.)

So he went to the kitchen to find Mom. "Mom, please come play with me," he said.

"Sorry, but I'm busy," said his mom. "Why don't you ask Bart?"

"I already did," said Nicky. (Remove Mom, put up Dad.)

Then he went to find his dad. "Dad, please come play with me."

"Sorry, but I'm busy now. Why don't you ask Bart?" (Remove Dad, put up Bart.)

So Nicky found Bart and said, "Mom and Dad can't play now. Will you play with me?"

Bart just looked at Nicky and sang:

"Nobody loves you.
Everybody hates you.

Go out to the garden and eat worms.
Big, fat, juicy ones,
Long, slim, slimy ones,
Oh, how they do squirm!"

Nicky frowned and went to find Grandpa. (Remove Bart, put up Grandpa.)
"Grandpa, please come play with me," he said.
"Sorry, but I'm busy now. Why don't you ask Bart?"
"He won't," said Nicky. (Remove Grandpa, put up Grandma.)
Nicky went to find Grandma instead. "Grandma, please come play with me," he said.
"Sorry, but I'm busy now. Why don't you ask Bart?" (Remove Grandma, put up Bart.)
So Nicky found Bart again and said, "Grandpa and Grandma can't play. Will you play with me?"
Bart smiled at Nicky and sang:

"Nobody loves you.
Everybody hates you.
Go out to the garden and eat worms.
Big, fat, juicy ones,
Long, slim, slimy ones,
Oh, how they do squirm!"

Nicky scowled at Bart and went to find Sarah. (Remove Bart, put up Sarah.)
"Sarah, please come play with me," he said.
"Sorry, but I'm busy now. Why don't you ask Bart?"
"He's mean," said Nicky. (Remove Sarah, put up dog.)
Nicky went outside to find Digby. But Digby was busy chasing the neighbor's cat and he wouldn't play, either. (Remove dog, put up Bart.)
Nicky trudged back into the house. Bart was waiting by the door. "Sarah and Digby wouldn't play with you either, huh?" Then he sang:

"Nobody loves you.
Everybody hates you.
Go out to the garden and eat worms.
Big, fat, juicy ones,
Long, slim, slimy ones,
Oh, how they do squirm!"

Nicky stomped into the kitchen. (Remove Bart, put up all other pieces) "In case anybody wants to know, I am going out to the garden." Then he sadly sang:

"Nobody loves me.
Everybody hates me.
I'm going to the garden to eat worms.
Big, fat, juicy ones,
Long, slim, slimy ones,
Oh, how they do squirm!"

"I love you," said Mom.

"No, you don't," said Nicky.

Mom smiled, "Yes, I do. I love you with my lips."

"Your lips?" said Nicky in a puzzled voice.

"Sure, I show I love you with my lips when I kiss you."

Then Dad said, "I love you with my arms every time I hug you."

"And I love you with my hand and my eye," said Grandpa.

"Huh," said Nicky.

"I'm saying 'I love you' with my hand whenever I ruffle your hair, and with my eye when I wink at you."

Then Grandma said, "I love you with my lap when I let you sit on it—even though you are getting pretty big."

"And I show I love you whenever we rub noses," said Sarah.

"And Digby loves you," said Mom. "He loves you with his tongue whenever he licks you, and with his tail when it wags."

"I guess," said Nicky, "but Bart doesn't love me."

"Yes, Bart loves you," said Dad. "He might not show it with hugs or kisses or winks, but he shows it in other ways." (Put up Bart.)

Just then, Bart came into the kitchen. "Hey, Nick-Buddy, Tyler and I are going fishing with his dad. Do you want to come along?"

Nicky grinned.

"Yes, but I have to go somewhere first."

"Where?" asked Bart.

"To the garden,"

Bart looked at Nicky.

"You know I was just kidding about that worm thing, don't you?"

"Yeah, but if you want to go fishing, you have to get . . ."

"Worms," said Bart with a laugh. And he and Nicky headed out of the house singing:

"Going to the garden to get worms.
Big, fat, juicy ones,
Long, slim, slimy ones,
Oh, how they do squirm!"

## Tips

- The refrain is track 62 on the CD.
- Photocopy and color the visuals provided to make the pieces. Teach the children the refrain before you start the story. The children can also participate by showing the different ways people demonstrate their love.

## Picture Book Pairings

Carr, Jan. *Sweet Hearts*. Illustrated by Dorothy Donohue. Holiday House, 2002. A young girl celebrates Valentine's Day by making and hiding paper hearts around the house for her family to discover. (Valentine's Day)

Hines, Anna Grossnickle. *Whose Shoes?* Illustrated by LeUyen Pham. Harcourt, 2001. A mouse tries on the shoes of various family members, from Daddy's great big clompy shoes and Mommy's clappy high-heeled shoes to those of Brother and Baby, but only one pair is just right. (Family)

Wild, Margaret. *Kiss Kiss!* Illustrated by Bridget Strevens-Marzo. Simon & Schuster, 2004. Baby Hippo is in such a rush to play one morning, he forgets to kiss his mama; but strangely, all the jungle noises seem to remind him. (Love)

**Figure 5-24   Nicky**     **Figure 5-25   Mom #2**     **Figure 5-26   Dad**     **Figure 5-27   Grandpa**

**Figure 5-28   Grandma**     **Figure 5-29   Sarah**     **Figure 5-30   Bart**     **Figure 5-31   Dog #3**

## STORY SONGS

A musical version of *Goldilocks and the Three Bears* was the first story song that I used in a program. I heard it from a kindergarten teacher; however, I think it is a camp song. After using it successfully, I challenged myself to write a story song. The result was "The Little Red Hen." "Tiny Tina" is my version of a commonly found theme in children's stories, about wanting "just one more thing."

### 1. LITTLE RED HEN

**Words and Music by Susan M. Dailey**          **Suggested themes: Chickens (Birds), Farms, Food**

CD Track 63

#### Pieces Needed

- Little Red Hen
- Mouse
- Cat
- Dog
- Hog

Once upon a time,
a long, long, long, long, long, long time ago,
there lived in a house
a little red hen (*Put pieces up as mentioned*) and a mouse,
a cat and a dog
and even a lazy hog.
Now I'll give you the scoop
of what happened to this group.

One day the little red hen said,
"I have a craving for some bread."
So she found herself some seed
to grow the wheat that she would need.

And she said, (*spoken*)

"Who will, who will help me
plant this seed?"
And the mouse said,
"Not I," (*in squeaky voice*)
and the cat said,
"No way," (*emphatically*)
and the dog said,
"Not now," (*Yawn and stretch.*)
And the hog said,
"No, no, never, never, uh, uh, uh!"

"Then, I'll just have to do it myself," said the Hen.
And she did!

The weather for growing plants was fine—
a little rain and plenty of sunshine.
Soon the seeds that she had sown
sprouted, and when they had grown,

Then she said, (*spoken*)

"Who will, who will help me
cut this wheat?"
And the mouse said,
"Not I,"
and the cat said,
"No way,"
and the dog said,
"Not now,"
and the hog said,
"No, no, never, never, uh, uh, uh!"

"Then I'll just have to do it myself," said the Hen.
And she did!

When all the wheat was cut down,
the hen took it to the mill in town.
She had to wait for an hour
while the miller ground her wheat into flour.

Then she said, (*spoken*)

"Who will, who will help me
Make the dough?"
And the mouse said,
"Not I,"
and the cat said,
"No way,"
and the dog said,
"Not now,"
and the hog said,
"No, no, never, never, uh, uh, uh!"

"Then I'll just have to do it myself," said the Hen.
And she did!

Into the kitchen she did go.
She mixed and kneaded the dough.

When the bread had baked for a spell,
from the kitchen came a wonderful smell!

And she said, (*spoken*)

"Who will, who will help me
eat this bread?"
And the mouse said,
"I will,"
and the cat said,
"Me, too,"
and the dog said,
"Right now,"
and the hog said,
"Yes, yes, always, always, yum, yum, yum!"
"No, you won't!" said the Little Red Hen.
And they didn't.

Once upon a time,
a long, long, long, long, long, long time ago,
there lived in a house
a little red hen and a mouse,
a cat and a dog
and even a helpful hog.
From this day, forever more,
they all helped with the chores.

## Tips

- The song is track 63 on the CD.
- Photocopy and color the visuals provided to make the pieces. I leave the pieces up during the entire song and just point to them when they speak. I add hand motions to the song when appropriate, e.g. move hands upward when wheat grows, make cutting motion when Hen cuts wheat, knead dough, etc.
- Teach the children the refrain before you start the story. When you get to the stanza where the animals want to eat the bread, teach the children the new words and have them repeat them.

## Picture Book Pairings

Kutner, Merrily. *Down on the Farm*. Illustrated by Will Hillenbrand. Holiday House, 2004. Simple rhyming text describes the sounds and activities of animals during a day on the farm. (Farms)

Paye, Won-Ldy. *Mrs. Chicken and the Hungry Crocodile*. Illustrated by Julie Paschkis. Holt, 2003. When a crocodile captures Mrs. Chicken and takes her to an island to fatten her up, clever Mrs. Chicken claims that she can prove they are sisters and that, therefore, the crocodile shouldn't eat her. (Chickens)

Sturges, Philemon. *The Little Hen Makes a Pizza*. Illustrated by Amy Walrod. Dutton, 1999. In this version of the traditional tale, the duck, the dog, and the cat refuse to help the Little Red Hen make a pizza but do get to participate when the time comes to eat it. (Food, Chickens)

Figure 5-32    Little Red Hen

Figure 5-33    Mouse #2

Figure 5-34    Cat #5

Figure 5-35    Dog #4

Figure 5-36    Hog

## 2. TINY TINA

**Words and Music by Susan M. Dailey**          **Suggested themes: Bedtime, Toys/Playing**

### Pieces Needed

- Bed
- Tina
- Teddy bears
- Dolls
- Cats
- Dogs
- Clowns
- Balls

Now it's time to go to bed,
but tiny Tina won't lay down her head.
"I can't sleep," Tina said,
"Without some toys in bed!"

Tina wants a teddy bear.
If you have a teddy bear,

put your bear on the bed.
Now, Tina can sleep.

But, no! (*spoken*)

Tina wants a pretty doll.
If you have a pretty doll,
put your doll on the bed.
Now, Tina can sleep.

But, no! (*spoken*)

Now it's time to go to bed,
but tiny Tina can't lay down her head.
"I can't sleep," Tina said,
"Without more toys in bed!"

Tina wants a cuddly cat.
If you have a cuddly cat,
put your cat on the bed.
Now, Tina can sleep.

But, no! (*spoken*)

Tina wants a friendly dog.
If you have a friendly dog,
put your dog on the bed.
Now, Tina can sleep.

But, no! (*spoken*)

Now it's time to go to bed,
but tiny Tina can't lay down her head.
"I can't sleep," Tina said,
"Without more toys in bed!"

Tina wants a funny clown.
If you have a funny clown,
put your clown on the bed.
Now, Tina can sleep.

But, no! (*spoken*)

Tina wants a bouncing ball.
If you have a bouncing ball,
put your ball on the bed.
Now, Tina can sleep.

But, no! (*spoken*)

Now it's time to go to bed,
but tiny Tina can't lay down her head.
"I can't sleep! As you can see,"
"There is no room for me!"

Tina needs a place to sleep,
so her toys go in a heap
beside the bed upon the floor.
Now, Tina begins to snore!

### Tips

- The sheet music is on page 176.
- Using the patterns, make Tina and the bed, as well as several copies of each toy. Use the clown from "Something's Hiding in a Flower" on page 64.
- Pass the toys out to the audience before the song. The children should bring them up to the board at the appropriate time. During the last verse, push all the toys off the bed. Encourage the children to say the "But, no!" with you.

### Picture Book Pairings

Smith, Maggie. *Paisley*. Illustrated by author. Knopf, 2004. Tired of collecting dust in a toy store, a stuffed elephant named Paisley ventures out in search of his Special Someone. (Toys/Playing)

Yolen, Jane. *How Do Dinosaurs Say Good Night?* Illustrated by Mark Teague. Blue Sky Press, 2000. Mother and child ponder the different ways a dinosaur can say goodnight, from slamming his tail and pouting to giving a big hug and kiss. (Bedtime)

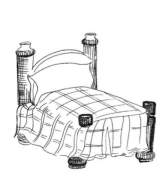

**Figure 5-37   Bed**

**Figure 5-38   Tina**

**Figure 5-39   Teddy Bear**

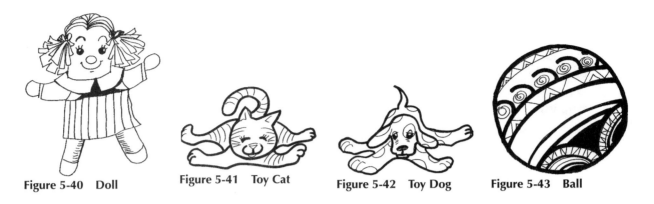

Figure 5-40    Doll          Figure 5-41    Toy Cat          Figure 5-42    Toy Dog          Figure 5-43    Ball

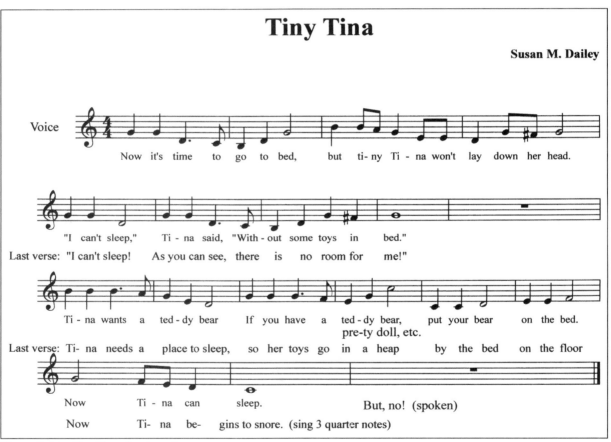

Figure 5-44    Tiny Tina sheet music

# CHAPTER 6

# SOURCES

## SOURCE A: "SINGABLE" PICTURE BOOKS

### Musical Refrains

Bryan, Ashley. *Beautiful Blackbird*. Illustrated by author. Atheneum, 2003. In a story of the Ila people, the colorful birds of Africa ask Blackbird, the most beautiful of birds, to decorate them with some of his "blackening brew." "Hush, Little Baby" is a possible tune for the songs in the story. (Suggested themes: Birds, Colors)

Denslow, Sharon Phillips. *Big Wolf and Little Wolf*. Illustrated by Cathie Felstead. Greenwillow, 2000. Grey wolf father and son sing to each other one night before being startled by noises in the bushes. "Yankee Doodle" is a possible tune for the songs in the story. (Suggested themes: Wolves, Families, Music, Bedtime)

Harper, Wilhelmina. *The Gunniwolf*. Illustrated by Barbara Upton. Dutton, 2003. A little girl cautioned never to go into the jungle wanders in deeper and deeper while searching for flowers—and is suddenly confronted by the gunniwolf. (Suggested themes: Music, Monsters)

Hest, Amy. *In the Rain with Baby Duck*. Illustrated by Jill Barton. Candlewick, 1995. Although her parents love walking in the rain, Baby Duck does not—until Grandpa shares a secret with her. "Hush, Little Baby" or "Jack and Jill" are possible tunes for the songs in the story. (Suggested themes: Ducks, Rain, Babies, Grandparents, Families)

Hurd, Thacher. *Mama Don't Allow: Starring Miles and the Swamp Band*. Illustrated by author. Harper-Collins, 1984. Miles and the Swamp Band have the time of their lives playing at the Alligator Ball, until they discover the menu includes Swamp Band soup. (Suggested themes: Music, Alligators)

Johnson, Paul Brett. *Little Bunny Foo Foo: Told and Sung by the Good Fairy*. Illustrated by author. Scholastic, 2004. In an adaptation of the children's song, the good fairy tells of her efforts to make the naughty bunny behave and what happens when these efforts fail. (Suggested themes: Rabbits, Nonsense)

Lester, Helen. *Tacky the Penguin*. Illustrated by Lynn Munsinger. Houghton Mifflin, 1988. Tacky the Penguin does not fit in with his sleek and graceful companions, but his odd behavior comes in handy when hunters come with maps and traps. (Suggested themes: Penguins, Birds, Winter)

MacDonald, Margaret Read. *Mabela the Clever*. Illustrated by Tim Coffey. Whitman, 2001. An African folktale about a mouse who pays close attention to her surroundings and avoids being tricked by the cat. (Suggested theme: Mice)

MacDonald, Margaret Read. *Pickin' Peas*. Illustrated by Pat Cummings. HarperCollins, 1998. Because a pesky rabbit picks peas from her garden, a little girl catches it and puts it in a box, but that doesn't solve the problem. (Suggested theme: Gardens, Rabbits)

Miranda, Anne. *To Market, to Market*. Illustrated by Janet Stevens. Harcourt, 1997. Starting with the nursery rhyme about buying a fat pig at market, this tale goes on to describe a series of unruly animals that run amok, evading capture and preventing the narrator from cooking lunch. (Suggested themes: Shopping, Food, Nonsense)

Robbins, Maria Polushkin. *Mother, Mother, I Want Another*. Illustrated by Jon Goodell. Knopf, 2005. In this newly illustrated edition, Mrs. Mouse is anxious to get her son to sleep and goes off to find what she thinks he wants. "Hush, Little Baby" is a possible tune for the songs in the story. (Suggested themes: Bedtime, Mice, Mothers)

Seeger, Pete. *Abiyoyo: Based on a South African Lullaby and Story*. Illustrated by Michael Hays. Macmillan, 1986. Banished from the town for making mischief, a little boy and his father are welcomed back when they find a way to make the dreaded giant Abiyoyo disappear. (Suggested themes: Magic, Monsters)

Seeger, Pete and Paul DuBois Jacobs. *Some Friends to Feed: The Story of Stone Soup*. Illustrated by Michael Hays. Putnam, 2005. A poor but clever traveler finds a way to get the townspeople to share their food with him in this retelling of a classic tale, set in Germany at the end of the Thirty Years War. (Suggested theme: Food)

Shannon, George. *Lizard's Song*. Illustrated by Jose Aruego and Ariane Dewey. Greenwillow, 1981. Bear tries repeatedly to learn Lizard's song. (Suggested themes: Music, Lizards, Bears, Reptiles)

Wheeler, Lisa. *Hokey Pokey: Another Prickly Love Story*. Illustrated by Janie Bynum. Little, Brown, 2006. After a series of discouraging dance teachers, Cushion the porcupine finds his rhythm with his true love, Barb. "Ten Little Indians" or "Hush, Little Baby" are possible tunes for the songs in the story. (Suggested themes: Dancing, Porcupines)

Wheeler, Lisa. *Porcupining: A Prickly Love Story*. Illustrated by Janie Bynum. Little, Brown, 2002. After a series of rejections, a lonely porcupine finds true love with a prickly hedgehog. "Yankee Doodle" is a possible tune for the songs in the story. (Suggested themes: Love, Feelings, Porcupines, Animals)

## Songs

Ajhar, Brian. *Home on the Range*. Illustrated by author. Dial, 2004. In this illustrated version of the familiar song, a young boy is transported from his city apartment to life on the range. (Suggested theme: Cowboys)

*All the Pretty Little Horses: A Traditional Lullaby*. Illustrated by Linda Saport. Clarion, 1999. A traditional lullaby presented with music, a note on the origin of the song, and pastel illustrations, which reflect its possible connection to slaves in the American South. (Suggested themes: Babies, Bedtime, Horses)

Arnold, Tedd. *Catalina Magdalena Hoopensteiner Wallendiner Hogan Logan Bogan Was Her Name*. Illustrated by author. Scholastic, 2004. Presents the words and music—and varying forms of the name—of a classic camp song that dates at least from the 1940s. (Suggested themes: Names, Nonsense, Body)

Autry, Gene. *Here Comes Santa Claus*. Illustrated by Bruce Whatley. HarperCollins, 2002. Santa Claus is riding down Santa Claus Lane tonight with toys for all girls and boys. (Suggested theme: Christmas)

Aylesworth, Jim. *The Completed Hickory Dickory Dock*. Illustrated by Eileen Christelow. Atheneum, 1990. Completes the classic nursery rhyme about the mouse that ran up the clock. (Suggested theme: Mice)

Bates, Ivan. *Five Little Ducks.* Illustrated by author. Scholastic, 2006. One by one, five little ducks wander away from their mother until her lonely quack brings them all waddling back. (Suggested themes: Ducks, Birds)

Bates, Katharine Lee. *America the Beautiful.* Illustrated by Wendell Minor. Putnam, 2003. An illustrated edition of the nineteenth-century poem, later set to music, celebrating the beauty of America. (Suggested themes: America, Fourth of July)

Bates, Katharine Lee. *America the Beautiful.* Illustrated by Chris Gall. Little, Brown, 2004. Four verses of the nineteenth-century poem, illustrated by the author's great-great-grandnephew. (Suggested themes: America, Fourth of July)

Beaumont, Karen. *I Ain't Gonna Paint No More!* Illustrated by David Catrow. Harcourt, 2005. In the rhythm of a familiar folk song, a child cannot resist adding one more dab of paint in surprising places. (Suggested theme: Art)

Berlin, Irving. *Easter Parade.* Illustrated by Lisa McCue. HarperCollins, 2003. In an illustrated version of the song, a little bunny and her father enjoy the Easter parade. (Suggested theme: Easter)

Berry, Holly. *Old MacDonald Has a Farm.* Illustrated by author. North-South Books, 1994. The inhabitants of Old MacDonald's farm are described, verse by verse. (Suggested themes: Farms, Animals, Sounds)

Bucchino, John. *Grateful: A Song of Giving Thanks.* Illustrated by Anna-Liisa Hakkarainen. HarperCollins, 2003. An illustrated version of John Bucchino's song of giving thanks and celebrating the gifts of life. (Suggested themes: Feelings, Thanksgiving)

Bunting, Eve. *Sing a Song of Piglets: A Calendar in Verse.* Illustrated by Emily Arnold McCully. Clarion, 2002. From skiing in January to surfing in July, two energetic piglets romp through the months of the year in this calendar in verse. (Suggested themes: Calendar, Pigs)

Butler, John. *Ten in the Den.* Illustrated by author. Peachtree, 2005. One by one, nine forest cratures fall out of bed when Little Mouse says, "Roll over." (Suggested themes: Bedtime, Animals)

Cabrera, Jane. *If You're Happy and You Know It.* Illustrated by author. Holiday, 2005. An elephant, a monkey, and a giraffe join other animals to sing different verses of this popular song that encourages everyone to express their happiness through voice and movement. (Suggested themes: Feelings, Movement)

Canyon, Christopher. *John Denver's Sunshine on My Shoulders.* Illustrated by author. Dawn Publications, 2003. A picture book adaptation of John Denver's song, "Sunshine on my Shoulders," which celebrates the simple things in life, such as sunshine, being outdoors in the beauty of nature, and loving relationships. (Suggested theme: Feelings)

Carle, Eric. *Today Is Monday.* Illustrated by author. Philomel, 1993. Each day of the week brings a new food, until on Sunday all the world's children can come and eat it up. (Suggested themes: Food, Calendar)

Carter, David A. *If You're Happy and You Know It.* Illustrated by author. Scholastic, 1997. In a pop-up version of the traditional song, animals lead readers through many motions. (Suggested themes: Feelings, Movement)

Child, Lydia Maria Francis. *Over the River and Through the Wood.* Illustrated by David Catrow. Holt, 1996. An illustrated version of the poem that became a well-known song about a journey through the snow to grandfather's house for Thanksgiving dinner. (Suggested theme: Thanksgiving)

Crum, Shutta. *The House in the Meadow.* Illustrated by Paige Billin-Frye. Whitman, 2003. In the year following a couple's marriage surrounded by their ten best friends, different sized crews of construction workers build a house for them, from nine strong diggers to one inspector. (Suggested themes: Construction, Houses, Counting)

*Dem Bones.* Illustrated by Bob Barner. Chronicle, 1996. A rendition of a traditional African American spiritual. (Suggested theme: Body)

*Do Your Ears Hang Low? A Love Story.* Illustrated by Caroline Jayne Church. Scholastic, 2002. Two long-eared dogs celebrate their love to the words of a familiar children's song. (Suggested themes: Dogs, Nonsense)

Eagle, Kin. *Hey, Diddle Diddle.* Illustrated by Rob Gilbert. Whispering Coyote Press, 1997. This expanded version of the traditional rhyme shows what happened after the cow jumped over the moon. (Suggested theme: Nonsense)

Eagle, Kin. *Humpty Dumpty.* Illustrated by Rob Gilbert. Whispering Coyote Press, 1999. This expanded version of the traditional rhyme presents the further misadventures of Humpty Dumpty after his original tumble off the wall. (Suggested themes: Eggs, Toys, Royalty)

Eagle, Kin. *It's Raining, It's Pouring.* Illustrated by Rob Gilbert. Whispering Coyote Press, 1998. This expanded version of the traditional rhyme shows what happens to the old man in all kinds of weather. (Suggested themes: Weather, Rain)

Eagle, Kin. *Rub a Dub Dub.* Illustrated by Rob Gilbert. Whispering Coyote Press, 1999. This expanded version of the traditional rhyme shows what happens to the butcher, the baker, and the candlestick maker when they go fishing in their tub. (Suggested themes: Fish, Nonsense)

Feliciano, José. *Feliz Navidad! Two Stories Celebrating Christmas.* Illustrated by David Diaz. Scholastic, 2003. The Caldecott winning illustrator depicts scenes from a *parranda,* a Christmas tradition in Puerto Rico, accompany this bilingual song. (Suggested theme: Christmas)

Fitzgerald, Ella and Van Alexander. *A-Tisket, A-Tasket.* Illustrated by Ora Eitan. Philomel, 2003. A boy in New York City drops his green and yellow basket and later sees a little girl carrying it around. (Suggested themes: Feelings, Baskets)

Fleming, Denise. *The First Day of Winter.* Illustrated by author. Holt, 2005. A snowman comes alive as the child building it adds pieces during the first ten days of winter. (Suggested theme: Winter)

Galdone, Paul. *Cat Goes Fiddle-I-Fee.* Illustrated by author. Clarion, 1985. An old English rhyme names all the animals a farm boy feeds on his daily rounds. (Suggested themes: Animals, Sounds, Farms)

Garriel, Barbara S. *I Know a Shy Fellow Who Swallowed a Cello.* Illustrated by John O'Brien. Boyds Mills Press, 2004. An adaptation of the folk rhyme "There Was an Old Woman Who Swallowed a Fly," featuring musical instruments. (Suggested theme: Music)

Gill, Jim. *May There Always Be Sunshine: A Traditional Song.* Illustrated by Susie Signorino-Richards. Jim Gill Books, 2001. Expands upon the traditional song with suggestions offered by children at the author's concerts. (Suggested theme: Feelings)

Goodman, Steve. *The Train They Call the City of New Orleans.* Illustrated by Michael McCurdy. Putnam, 2003. An illustrated version of the familiar song about riding on a train called the City of New Orleans. (Suggested theme: Trains)

Guthrie, Woody. *This Land Is Your Land.* Illustrated by Kathy Jakobsen. Little, Brown, 1998. This well-known folk song is accompanied by a tribute from folksinger Pete Seeger, the musical notation, and a biographical scrapbook with photographs. (Suggested themes: America, Fourth of July)

Hale, Sarah Josepha Buell. *Mary Had a Little Lamb.* Illustrated by Sally Mavor. Orchard, 1995. Fabric relief illustrations accompany this familiar nursery rhyme about a young girl whose lamb follows her to school. Includes information about the history of the rhyme. (Suggested themes: Sheep, School)

Harper, Cherise Mericle. *Itsy Bitsy the Smart Spider.* Illustrated by author. Dial, 2004. The spider from the famous nursery rhyme gets a job in order to buy a cover that will keep her dry and prevent her being washed down the water spout again. (Suggested themes: Spiders, Rain, Jobs)

Harper, Cherise Mericle. *There Was a Bold Lady Who Wanted a Star.* Illustrated by author. Little, Brown, 2002. In this variation on the traditional cumulative rhyme, a feisty woman tries roller skates, a bicycle, and even a rocket to reach a star. (Suggested themes: Moon & Stars, Shopping, Vehicles)

Harter, Debbie. *The Animal Boogie.* Illustrated by author. Barefoot, 2000. In the jungle, the animals' toes are twitching, their bodies are wiggling, and their wings are flapping—as they teach children how to do the Animal Boogie. (Suggested themes: Movement, Animals, Jungle)

Hillenbrand, Will. *Down by the Station.* Illustrated by author. Harcourt, 1999. In this version of a familiar song, baby animals ride to the children's zoo on the zoo train. (Suggested themes: Zoo, Trains)

Hillenbrand, Will. *Fiddle-I-Fee.* Illustrated by author. Harcourt, 2002. In this cumulative nursery rhyme, a farmer and his wife prepare for a new baby as their animals secretly meet at night to plan a surprise of their own. (Suggested themes: Music, Animals)

Hillenbrand, Will. *Here We Go Round the Mulberry Bush.* Illustrated by author. Harcourt, 2003. A traditional nursery song is expanded to tell the story of a young child's first day at school. (Suggested theme: School)

Hoberman, Mary Ann. *Bill Grogan's Goat.* Illustrated by Nadine Bernard Westcott. Little, Brown, 2002. Presents the familiar rhyme about a pesky goat that gets in trouble for eating shirts off the clothesline. (Suggested themes: Goats, Clothes)

Hoberman, Mary Ann. *The Eensy Weensy Spider.* Illustrated by Nadine Bernard Westcott. Little, Brown, 2000. An expanded version of the familiar children's song describing what the little spider does after being washed out of the water-spout. (Suggested themes: Spiders, Bugs)

Hoberman, Mary Ann. *Mary Had a Little Lamb.* Illustrated by Nadine Bernard Westcott. Little, Brown, 2003. This expanded version of the traditional rhyme shows what happens after the lamb gets to school. (Suggested themes: Sheep, School)

Hoberman, Mary Ann. *Miss Mary Mack.* Illustrated by Nadine Bernard Westcott. Little, Brown, 1998. An expanded adaptation of the familiar hand-clapping rhyme about a young girl and an elephant. (Suggested theme: Elephants)

Hoberman, Mary Ann. *Yankee Doodle.* Illustrated by Nadine Bernard Westcott. Little, Brown, 2004. Expands on the familiar song to include a girl, a poodle, a toad, and a rooster who, along with Yankee Doodle, open a restaurant called Yankee Doodle's Noodles. (Suggested themes: Food, Fourth of July)

Hort, Lenny. *Seals on the Bus.* Illustrated by G. Brian Karas. Holt, 2000. Different animals—including seals, tigers, geese, rabbits, monkeys, and more—make their own sounds as they ride all around the town on a bus. (Suggested themes: Buses, Vehicles, Animals, Sounds)

*Hush Little Baby.* Illustrated by Marla Frazee. Browndeer Press, 1999. In an old lullaby a baby is promised an assortment of presents from its adoring parent. (Suggested theme: Babies)

Jackson, Alison. *The Ballad of Valentine.* Illustrated by Tricia Tusa. Dutton, 2002. An ardent suitor tries various means of communication, from smoke signals to Morse code to skywriting, in order to get his message to his Valentine. (Suggested theme: Valentine's Day)

Jackson, Alison. *I Know an Old Lady Who Swallowed a Pie.* Illustrated by Judith Byron Schachner. Dutton, 1997. An old lady comes to dinner, but ends up in the Thanksgiving parade. (Suggested theme: Thanksgiving)

Keats, Ezra Jack. *Over in the Meadow.* Illustrated by author. Viking, 1999. An old nursery poem introduces animals and their young and the numbers one through ten. (Suggested themes: Counting, Animals, Babies, Mothers)

Kellogg, Steven. *Santa Claus Is Comin' to Town.* Illustrated by author. HarperCollins, 2004. The 1930's song by J. Fred Coots and Haven Gillespie is brought to life. (Suggested theme: Christmas)

Kennedy, Jimmy. *The Teddy Bears' Picnic.* Illustrated by Michael Hague. Holt, 1992. A newly-illustrated version of the song about teddy bears picnicking independently of their "owners." (Suggested themes: Picnics, Teddy Bears, Toys)

Kovalski, Maryann. *The Wheels on the Bus.* Illustrated by author. Joy Street, 1987. While a grandmother and grandchildren wait for the bus, they sing the title song with such gusto they miss their bus. (Suggested themes: Buses, Grandparents, Families, Shopping)

Kubler, Annie. *Row, Row, Row Your Boat.* Illustrated by author. Child's Play, 2003. An illustrated board book with words and music to a children's song. (Suggested themes: Boats, Vehicles)

Langstaff, John. *Frog Went a-Courtin'.* Illustrated by Feodor Rojankovsky. Harcourt, 1955. Frog is looking for a bride. (Suggested themes: Frogs, Love, Valentine's Day)

Langstaff, John. *Oh, a-Hunting We Will Go.* Illustrated by Nancy Winslow Parker. Aladdin Books, 1991. Old and new verses for a popular folk song about hunting and capturing an animal—and then letting him go. (Suggested themes: Animals, Nonsense)

Lewis, E. B. *This Little Light of Mine.* Illustrated by author. Simon & Schuster, 2005. A young boy brings friendship and happiness where he goes. (Suggested themes: Friends, Feelings)

Lithgow, John. *Marsupial Sue.* Illustrated by Jack E. Davis. Simon & Schuster, 2001. Marsupial Sue, a young kangaroo, finds happiness in doing what kangaroos do. (Suggested themes: Kangaroos, Feelings)

Loesser, Frank. *I Love You! A Bushel & A Peck.* Illustrated by Rosemary Wells. HarperCollins, 2005. A farmer duck declares his feelings and even wonders how he'll take care of his farm because he wants to be with his love. (Suggested themes: Love, Ducks)

MacDonald, Margaret Read. *A Hen, a Chick, and a String Guitar.* Illustrated by Sophie Fatus. Barefoot Books, 2005. A cumulative tale from Chile that begins with a hen and ends with sixteen different animals and a guitar. (Suggested themes: Pets, Animals, Sounds, Counting, Music, Dancing)

Mallett, David. *Inch by Inch: The Garden Song.* Illustrated by Ora Eitan. HarperCollins, 1995. Inch by inch, row by row, a child grows a garden with the help of the rain and the earth. Based on a popular folksong. (Suggested theme: Gardens)

Manders, John. *Señor Don Gato: A Traditional Song.* Illustrated by author. Candlewick, 2003. When he climbs on a roof to read a love letter, a cat has an unfortunate fall with unexpected consequences. Music and Spanish translation at back of book. (Suggested themes: Cats, Mexico)

Manning, Maurie. *The Aunts Go Marching.* Illustrated by author. Boyds Mills Press, 2003. Dressed in raincoats and carrying umbrellas, a platoon of aunts march through the rainy city streets led by a little girl with a drum in this cumulative rhyme. (Suggested themes: Rain, Families, Counting)

Marsh, T. J. and Jennifer Ward. *Way Out in the Desert.* Illustrated by Kenneth J. Spengler. Rising Moon, 1998. A counting book in rhyme presents various desert animals and their children, from a mother horned toad and her little toadie one to a mom tarantula and her little spiders ten. Numerals are hidden in each illustration. (Suggested themes: Deserts, Counting, Animals, Babies, Mothers)

Nelson, Steve and Jack Rollins. *Frosty the Snowman.* Illustrated by Richard Cowdrey. Grosset & Dunlap, 2003. An illustrated version of the familiar song in which a snowman, who was brought to life by an old silk hat, has great fun playing with the children who built him. (Suggested theme: Winter)

Newman, Lesléa. *The Eight Nights of Chanukah.* Illustrated by Elivia Savadier. Abrams, 2005. The wondrous days of Chanukah come to life through the eyes of a young child, whose family gathering grows bigger and bigger as the holiday progresses. (Suggested theme: Hanukkah)

Norworth, Jack. *Take Me out to the Ballgame.* Illustrated by Alec Gillman. Four Winds, 1993. The lyrics of the familiar song, illustrated by pictures based on the World Series games played between the Dodgers and the Yankees in 1949 in Ebbets Field. (Suggested themes: Baseball, Games, Summer)

O'Brien, John. *The Farmer in the Dell.* Illustrated by author. Boyds Mills Press, 2000. An illustrated version of the traditional children's rhyme. (Suggested theme: Farms)

Ormerod, Jan. *Ms. MacDonald Has a Class.* Illustrated by author. Clarion, 1996. After visiting the farm, the children in Ms. MacDonald's class learn to move and look and sound very different while preparing to present the performance of a lifetime. (Suggested theme: School)

Owen, Ann. *Ants Go Marching.* Illustrated by Sandra D'Antonio. Picture Window Books, 2003. Presents an illustrated version of the traditional song along with some discussion of its folk origins. (Suggested themes: Bugs, Picnics)

Owen, Ann. *Old MacDonald Had a Farm.* Illustrated by Sandra D'Antonio. Picture Window Books, 2003. Presents an illustrated version of the traditional song along with some discussion of its folk origins. (Suggested themes: Farms, Animals, Sounds)

Paxton, Tom. *Going to the Zoo.* Illustrated by Karen Lee Schmidt. Morrow, 1996. Enthusiastic siblings describe the animals at the "zoo, zoo, zoo." (Suggested theme: Zoo)

Peek, Merle. *Mary Wore Her Red Dress, and Henry Wore His Green Sneakers.* Illustrated by author. Clarion, 1985. Each of Katy Bear's animal friends wears a different color of clothing to her birthday party. (Suggested themes: Colors, Clothes, Birthdays)

Peek, Merle. *Roll Over! A Counting Song.* Illustrated by author. Clarion, 1981. Before going to sleep a little boy keeps rolling over and as he does the ten imaginary animals that are crowded into the bed with him fall out one after the other. (Suggested themes: Bedtime, Counting, Animals)

Penner, Fred. *The Cat Came Back.* Illustrated by Renée Reichert. Roaring Brook Press, 2005. A persistent and indestructible cat keeps coming back, despite his owner's attempts to give him away. (Suggested theme: Cats)

Pinkney, J. Brian. *Hush Little Baby.* Illustrated by author. Greenwillow, 2006. An illustrated version of the traditional folk song in which a father promises the world to his restless baby daughter. (Suggested themes: Babies, Families)

Raffi. *Baby Beluga.* Illustrated by Ashley Wolff. Crown, 1992. Presents the illustrated text to the song about the little white whale who swims wild and free. (Suggested theme: Sea)

Raffi. *Down by the Bay.* Illustrated by Nadine Bernard Westcott. Crown, 1987. In this song, two children imagine their mothers asking, "Did you ever see a goose kissing a moose, a fly wearing a tie, or llamas eating their pajamas down by the bay?" (Suggested theme: Nonsense)

Raffi. *Five Little Ducks.* Illustrated by Jose Aruego and Ariane Dewey. Crown, 1989. When her five little ducks disappear one by one, Mother Duck sets out to find them. (Suggested themes: Ducks, Counting)

Raffi. *Shake My Sillies Out.* Illustrated by David Allender. Crown, 1987. Animals and campers join together in the woods one evening and shake their sillies, clap their crazies, and yawn their sleepies out. (Suggested themes: Bedtime, Camping, Movement, Nonsense)

*Rodgers and Hammerstein's My Favorite Things.* Illustrated by Rene Graef. HarperCollins, 2000. An illustrated version of the popular song enumerating favorite things, from raindrops on roses to silver-white winters melting into springs. (Suggested themes: Feelings, Love)

Rose, Deborah Lee. *The Twelve Days of Kindergarten.* Illustrated by Carey Armstrong-Ellis. Abrams, 2003. A cumulative counting verse in which a child enumerates items in the kindergarten classroom, from the whole alphabet, A to Z, to twelve eggs for hatching. (Suggested theme: School)

Russell, Bill. *Spider on the Floor.* Illustrated by True Kelley. Crown, 1993. Presents the illustrated text to the song about the curious spider. (Suggested themes: Spiders, Body)

Sherman, Allan and Lou Busch. *Hello Muddah, Hello Faddah: (A Letter from Camp).* Illustrated by Jack E. Davis. Dutton, 2004. A young camper writes to this parents begging to come home because camp is horrible. (Suggested theme: Camping)

Shulman, Lisa. *Old MacDonald Had a Workshop.* Illustrated by Ashley Wolff. Putnam, 2002. A female Old MacDonald builds a farm in her workshop. (Suggested themes: Farms, Toys, Construction, Sheep)

Sloat, Terri. *There Was an Old Lady Who Swallowed a Trout!* Illustrated by Reynold Ruffins. Holt, 1998. Set on the coast of the Pacific Northwest, this variation on the traditional cumulative rhyme describes the silly consequences of an old woman's fishy diet. (Suggested themes: Sea, Animals)

Sturges, Philemon. *She'll Be Comin' 'Round the Mountain.* Illustrated by Ashley Wolff. Little, Brown, 2004. New words to the traditional tune describe a camper-driving, "hootin' " and "shoutin' " guest and the party that will begin when she arrives. (Suggested themes: Books, Libraries, Animals)

Taback, Simms. *There Was an Old Lady Who Swallowed a Fly.* Illustrated by author. Viking, 1997. Presents the traditional version of a famous American folk poem first heard in the U.S. in the 1940's, with illustrations on die-cut pages that reveal all that the old lady swallows. (Suggested themes: Nonsense, Animals)

Taylor, Jane. *Twinkle, Twinkle, Little Star: A Traditional Lullaby.* Illustrated by Sylvia Long. Chronicle Books, 2001. The star shines on animals getting ready for bed. (Suggested themes: Bedtime, Animals, Moon & Stars)

Thornhill, Jan. *Over in the Meadow.* Illustrated by author. Maple Tree Press, 2004. The traditional Appalachian counting rhyme is illustrated with collages created from everyday objects. (Suggested themes: Counting, Animals, Babies, Mothers)

Trapani, Iza. *Baa Baa Black Sheep.* Illustrated by author. Whispering Coyote, 2001. In this expanded version of the traditional nursery rhyme, the black sheep has a surprise for the other farm animals. (Suggested themes: Sheep, Animals, Food, Clothes)

Trapani, Iza. *Froggie Went a-Courtin'.* Illustrated by author. Whispering Coyote, 2002. An adaptation of the folk song about a frog in search of a bride. (Suggested themes: Frogs, Love, Valentine's Day)

Trapani, Iza. *How Much Is that Doggie in the Window?* Illustrated by author. Whispering Coyote, 2001. Longing to buy a special puppy, a boy tries to earn the money he needs but ends up spending it on family members, who ultimately surprise him with a special gift. (Suggested themes: Dogs, Pets, Families)

Trapani, Iza. *I'm a Little Teapot.* Illustrated by author. Whispering Coyote, 2000. Expanded verses of a familiar song tell how a teapot dreams of visiting China, Mexico, the opera, a jungle, and other places while waiting to be used to serve tea. (Suggested themes: Vacations/Traveling, World)

Trapani, Iza. *The Itsy Bitsy Spider.* Illustrated by author. Whispering Coyote, 1998. The itsy-bitsy spider encounters a fan, a mouse, a cat, and a rocking chair as she makes her way to the top of a tree to spin her web. (Suggested theme: Spiders)

Trapani, Iza. *Mary Had a Little Lamb.* Illustrated by author. Whispering Coyote, 2001. This expanded version of the traditional rhyme shows what happens when the lamb decides to go off alone. (Suggested themes: Sheep, Farms, Animals)

Trapani, Iza. *Oh Where, Oh Where Has My Little Dog Gone?* Illustrated by author. Whispering Coyote, 1998. An expanded version of the traditional rhyme, in which the little dog runs away and explores the desert, mountains, and oceans before deciding that home is best. (Suggested themes: Dogs, Vacations/Traveling)

Trapani, Iza. *Row, Row, Row Your Boat.* Illustrated by author. Whispering Coyote, 1999. This expanded version of the traditional singing rhyme shows what happens when a family of bears rows their boat down the stream. (Suggested themes: Bears, Boats, Vacation/Traveling)

Trapani, Iza. *Shoo Fly!* Illustrated by author. Whispering Coyote, 2000. This expanded version of the traditional rhyme shows what happens when a young mouse tries to get rid of a pesky fly. (Suggested themes: Flies, Bugs, Mice)

Trapani, Iza. *Twinkle, Twinkle, Little Star.* Illustrated by author. Whispering Coyote, 1998. An expanded version of the nineteenth-century poem in which a small girl accompanies a star on a journey through the night sky, examining both heavenly bodies and the earth below. (Suggested theme: Moon & Stars)

Tyler, Gillian. *Froggy Went a-Courtin'.* Illustrated by author. Candlewick, 2005. Illustrates the well-known folk song about the courtship and marriage of the frog and the mouse. (Suggested themes: Frogs, Love)

Wadsworth, Olive A. *Over in the Meadow: A Counting Rhyme.* Illustrated by Anna Vojtech. North-South, 2002. A variety of meadow animals pursuing their daily activities introduce the numbers one through ten. (Suggested themes: Counting, Animals, Babies, Mothers)

Ward, Jennifer. *Over in the Garden.* Illustrated by Kenneth J. Spengler. Rising Moon, 2002. Over in the garden, mother insects and their children enjoy various activities from morning sun to evening moon. (Suggested themes: Bugs, Counting)

Wells, Rosemary. *The Bear Went Over the Mountain.* Illustrated by author. Scholastic, 1998. A bear goes over the mountain and all he could see was the other side. (Suggested theme: Bears)

Wells, Rosemary. *Bingo.* Illustrated by author. Scholastic, 1999. An illustrated version of the children's song about a dog named Bingo. (Suggested themes: Dogs, Names)

Wells, Rosemary. *The Itsy-Bitsy Spider.* Illustrated by author. Scholastic, 1998. A duck watches as the itsy-bitsy spider goes up and down the water spout. (Suggested theme: Spiders)

Westcott, Nadine Bernard. *I Know an Old Lady Who Swallowed a Fly.* Illustrated by author. Little, Brown, 2003. A cumulative folk song in which the solution proves worse than the predicament when an old lady swallows a fly. (Suggested themes: Nonsense, Animals)

Westcott, Nadine Bernard. *The Lady with the Alligator Purse.* Illustrated by author. Little, Brown, 1988. The old jump rope/nonsense rhyme features an ailing young Tiny Tim. (Suggested themes: Sickness, Nonsense)

Westcott, Nadine Bernard. *Skip to My Lou.* Illustrated by author. Little, Brown, 1989. When his parents leave a young boy in charge of the farm for a day, chaos erupts as the animals take over the house. (Suggested themes: Farms, Dancing, Cleaning Up, Nonsense)

Whippo, Walt. *Little White Duck.* Illustrated by Joan Paley. Little, Brown, 2000. Based on the song of the same title, a little white duck causes a commotion in its pond. (Suggested themes: Ducks, Sounds)

Williams, Suzanne. *Old MacDonald in the City.* Illustrated by Thor Wickstrom. Golden Book, 2002. Increasing numbers of different animals, from one horse to ten ants, try to steal food from Old Mac-Donald's corner food cart. (Suggested themes: City, Counting, Food, Sounds, Animals)

Williams, Suzanne. *The Witch Casts a Spell.* Illustrated by Barbara Olsen. Dial, 2002. Sung to the tune of "The Farmer in the Dell," verses describe the activities on Halloween night. (Suggested theme: Halloween)

Zane, Alex. *The Wheels on the Race Car.* Illustrated by James Warhola. Orchard, 2005. Animal race car drivers roar around the track. Sing to "The Wheels on the Bus" tune. (Suggested theme: Cars)

Zelinksy, Paul O. *Knick-Knack Paddywhack!* Paper engineering by Andrew Baron. Dutton, 2002. A young boy sets out on a walk—pull the tabs and tiny old men from One to Ten act out the familiar refrain of the traditional counting song on and all around him. (Suggested themes: Counting, Nonsense)

Zelinsky, Paul O. *The Wheels on the Bus.* Paper engineering by Rodger Smith. Dutton, 1990. The wheels on the bus go round, the wipers go swish, the doors open and close, and the people go in and out in this movable book version of the classic song. (Suggested themes: Buses, Vehicles, Sounds)

## SOURCE B: RECOMMENDED RECORDINGS

Beale, Pamela Conn and Susan Hagen Nipp. *Wee Sing Silly Songs*. Price Stern Sloan, 1982.

Beale, Pamela Conn and Susan Hagen Nipp. *Wee Wee Sing Sing-alongs*. Price Stern Sloan, 2005.

Gill, Jim. *Irrational Anthem*. Jim Gill Music, 2001.

Gill, Jim. *Jim Gill Sings Do Re Mi on His Toe Leg Knee*. Jim Gill Music, 1999.

Gill, Jim. *Jim Gill Sings Moving Rhymes for Modern Times*. Jim Gill Music, 2006.

Gill, Jim. *Jim Gill Sings the Sneezing Song and Other Contagious Tunes*. Jim Gill Music, 1993.

Greg & Steve. *Playing Favorites*. Youngheart, 1991.

Jenkins, Ella. *Songs Children Love to Sing*. Smithsonian/Folkways Records, 1996.

McGrath, Bob. *Sing along with Bob. #1* by Bob McGrath. Golden Books, 1996.

*More Sunday Morning Songs with Bob & Larry: VeggieTales Sing-Alongs*. Big Idea Records, 2005.

Palmer, Hap. *Early Childhood Classics: Old Favorites with a New Twist*. Hap-Pal Music, 2000.

Peter, Paul and Mary. *Peter, Paul and Mommy*. Warner, 1990.

Raffi. *The Corner Grocery Store*. Shoreline Records, 1979.

Raffi. *More Singable Songs for the Very Young*. Shoreline, 1977.

Raffi. *Raffi's Box of Sunshine*. Shoreline Records, 2000.

Raffi. *Singable Songs for the Very Young*. Shoreline, 1976.

Scruggs, Joe. *Late Last Night*. Educational Graphics Press, 1984.

Sharon, Lois and Bram. *Mainly Mother Goose*. Elephant Records, 1994.

Wonder Kids Choir. *101 Sing-a-Longs for Kids*. TimeLife, 2000.

Wonder Kids Choir. *Ultimate Kids Song Collection: 101 Favorite Sing-a-Longs, volumes 1–3*. Madacy Entertainment Group, 2000.

## SOURCE C: RESOURCES FOR PROGRAM PLANNING

### Books

*1001 Rhymes & Fingerplays for Working with Young Children*. Warren Publishing House, Inc., 1994.

Benton, Gail and Trisha Waichulaitis. *Low-Cost, High-Interest Programming: Seasonal Events for Preschoolers*. Neal-Schuman, 2004.

Benton, Gail and Trisha Waichulaitis. *Ready-to-Go Storytimes: Fingerplays, Scripts, Patterns, Music, and More*. Neal-Schuman, 2003.

*Big Book of Children's Songs*. Hal Leonard, 1988.

Cobb, Jane. *I'm a Little Teapot!: Presenting Preschool Storytime*. Black Sheep Press, 1996.

Cole, Joanna and Stephanie Calmenson, comp. *The Eentsy, Weentsy Spider: Fingerplays and Action Rhymes*. Illustrated by Alan Tiegreen. Morrow, 1991.

Costello, Elaine. *Random House Webster's Concise American Sign Language Dictionary*. Illustrated by Lois Lenderman, Paul M. Setzer and Linda C. Tom. Bantam, 2002.

Dailey, Susan M. *A Storytime Year: A Month-to-month Kit for Preschool Programming*. Neal-Schuman, 2001.

Glazer, Tom. *Tom Glazer's Treasury of Songs for Children*. Illustrated by John O'Brien. Doubleday, 1988.

Gustason, Gerilee and Esther Zawolkow. *Signing Exact English*. Illustrations by Lilian Lopez. Modern Signs Press, 1993

Katz, Alan. *I'm Still Here in the Bathtub: Brand New Silly Dilly Songs*. Illustrated by David Catrow. McElderry, 2003.

Katz, Alan. *Take Me out of the Bathtub and Other Silly Dilly Songs*. Illustrated by David Catrow. McElderry, 2001.

*Library Sparks*. Highsmith, 2003.

Lima, Carolyn W. and John A. Lima. *A to Zoo: Subject Access to Children's Picture Books*. 7th edition. Bowker, 2006.

MacDonald, Margaret Read. *Shake-it-up Tales! Stories to Sing, Dance, Drum, and Act Out*. August House, 2000.

Newcome, Zita. *Head, Shoulders, Knees, and Toes: And Other Action Counting Rhymes*. Candlewick, 2002.

Orozco, José Luis. *Diez Deditos: Ten Little Fingers and Other Play Rhymes and Action Songs from Latin America*. Illustrated by Elisa Kleven. Dutton, 1997.

Schiller, Pam and Thomas Moore. *Where Is Thumbkin?: Over 500 Activities to Use with Songs You Already Know*. Illustrated by Cheryl Kirk Noll. Gryphon House, 1993.

Stetson, Emily. *Little Hands Fingerplays & Action Songs: Seasonal Activities & Creative Play for 2- to 6-year-olds*. Williamson, 2001.

Warren, Jean, comp. *The Best of Totline Newsletter*. Warren Publishing House, 1995.

Yolen, Jane, ed. *This Little Piggy and Other Rhymes to Sing and Play*. Illustrated by Will Hillenbrand. Candlewick, 2005.

### Internet Sites

*American Sign Language Browser* from Michigan State University. http://commtechlab.msu.edu/sites/aslweb/browser.htm

*Bay View ACL Storytime Ideas*. www.bayviews.org/storytime.html

*Best Books for Kids*. www.thebestkidsbooksite.com

*Books to Grow On*. www.kcls.org/webkids/btgo/index.cfm

*DLTK's Printable Crafts*. www.dltk-kids.com

*Dr. Jean Feldman*. http://drjean.org

*Enchanted Learning*. www.enchantedlearning.com/Home.html

*Hummingbird Educational Resources*. www.hummingbirded.com

*KIDiddles*. http://kididdles.com/mouseum/alpha.html

*My Storytime*. www.geocities.com/mystorytime/themes.htm

*PUBYAC*. www.pubyac.org

*Step by Step Theme Pages*. http://stepbystepcc.com/themes.html

*Storytime Ideas*. www.ula.org/organization/rt/csrt/csrt-storytm.htm

*Susan M. Dailey*. www.susanmdailey.com

# Index of Picture Book Titles

# Index of Storytime Themes

# Index of Picture Book Authors

# About the Illustrator

Nancy Carroll Wagner's degree in studio art from Saint Mary of the Woods College was the natural result of her lifelong interest in creativity. She was zoo artist for six summers at the Children's Zoo in Fort Wayne, Indiana.

At the start of her professional career, Nancy lived and worked in New York City as an illustrator for Harcourt Brace & Jovanovich Publishers. In 1975, creative endeavors led her and her husband Steven to London, where she completed courses at the Sir John Cass School of Art and the University of London.

Nancy works as a freelance artist and has created murals in 100 schools, as well as libraries and churches in Indiana, Illinois, Ohio, Michigan and Florida. She is a frequent teacher at workshops and courses. In addition, Nancy has fulfilled several artist-in-residence positions.

She and her husband are the parents of four sons—the oldest, a U.S. Navy pilot, and the youngest, an elementary student. Her home welcomes a host of fortunate pets, reflecting Nancy's lifelong interest in animals and wildlife.

# About the Author

Susan M. Dailey is the author of *A Storytime Year,* which was published by Neal-Schuman in 2001. She has more than 30 years of library experience, starting as a high school page. Susan is a branch manager in the Wells County Public Library system, in northeast Indiana.

Since the publication of *A Storytime Year*, Susan has presented workshops in Indiana, Kentucky, Illinois, Wisconsin, and Arizona. She was chair of the Children's and Young People's Division of the Indiana Library Federation in 1994.

Susan and her husband, Doug, are the parents of three grown children—a daughter and two sons. In 2005, her older son and daughter-in-law provided a grandson with whom Susan can share her songs.

Susan maintains a website, www.susanmdailey.com, where she shares some of her new material. Many of Susan's songs and stories were written in her car. She hopes that people she passes think she's singing along with the radio!